DECORATIVE TOUCHES

35 Step-by-step Projects

CREATIVE PUBLISHING international

Minnetonka, Minnesota

Table *of* Contents

Wood Works

*A*nything made of wood will add a sense of solidity and permanency to your home. Natural wood tones lend warmth and beauty when the intricacy of its grain remains visible. Wood furnishings can blend with or enhance the original architecture of a home while they conceal unattractive features, or while they provide privacy or storage space. Smaller wooden accessories provide us with opportunities to delight in the unusual.

Construct beautiful architectural details by adding wood floors, wall frames, alcove cupboards and radiator covers. Install cornices and shutters to accentuate your windows. Create something totally unexpected by decorating your favorite old pieces of furniture, or by assembling a new light fixture. Follow the step-by-step instructions and photographs in this section to success.

WOOD-STRIP FLOORS

*Give your room the luxurious look of a solid
wood floor without the expense by laying hardwearing
and stylish wood-strip flooring.*

Pergo laminate flooring

Wood-strip flooring is hard wearing and smart and will complement most decorative schemes within your home. It offers the look of a solid wood floor without the mess and inconvenience of sanding and varnishing existing floorboards, and it's so easy to lay that an entire room can be completed in one day, without the need to use expensive or complicated equipment.

The strips are tongued and grooved to make installation easy with perfect joints. The finished floor simply 'floats' above the existing floor and is not attached to it. The boards are glued or clipped to each other, not the floor underneath, to form a detached layer resting on top of a polystyrene foam underlay. Spacers are provided to create a gap around the edge of the floor to allow for expansion in humid conditions. When the floor is complete the gap is concealed with molding. Once the floor has been laid it is ready to use and needs no further finishing,

▲ *Give your home a contemporary feel with the clean lines of a wood-strip floor. A practical alternative to carpet and quicker to lay than floor tiles, wood-strip boards look stylish in any room.*

and providing it is cared for, it will look good for many years. The strips are available in a number of different wood effects to suit all needs.

The instructions show how to install a wood-strip floor using the glue technique.

LAYING A WOOD-STRIP FLOOR

There are three different types of wood-strip flooring, each with its own advantages, and you will need to decide which is the most appropriate for your needs before you buy.

Laminated wood-strip flooring is the most economical purchase. The boards themselves are made of fiberboard, and this is coated with a thin layer of plastic that has been photographically printed to look like wood. It resists stains and moisture damage, and is best suited for kitchens and bedrooms.

Veneered wood-strip flooring is a slightly more costly alternative. Instead of a layer of plastic it has a veneer of wood on the surface. The thicker the veneer, the more durable the floor will be.

Solid wood-strip is the most expensive option, but it is also the most hardwearing and, if damaged, can be sanded down and re-finished many times. It is the only kind of wood-strip flooring that is hardwearing enough to be used in a very busy area such as a hallway.

➤ *A laminate floor would best suit an area of light to moderate use, such as a bedroom or general living area.*

Pergo laminate flooring

YOU WILL NEED

- Wood-strip flooring
- Underlay
- Hammer and nail set
- Screws and screwdriver
- Staple gun and staples
- Utility knife
- Spacers
- Wood glue
- Jigsaw with fine-tooth blade or tenon saw
- Plastic tamping block

- Damp cloth
- Pencil
- Profile gauge, optional
- Coping saw
- Medium-grade sandpaper
- Quarter-round molding
- Miter box and tenon saw
- Plank puller or small crowbar
- Drill and spade drill bits
- Finishing nails; panel nails

Before you start

Work out the floor area of your room in square yards (or square meters) and make a note of it. The area covered by a pack of flooring varies from brand to brand so ask the supplier for help in calculating the finished amount. Always add a little extra for waste and errors. Many of the tools you will need to lay the floor are available at flooring suppliers and home improvement centers.

PREPARING THE SURFACE

1 Use a nail set and hammer to drive all nail heads below the surface of the floorboards so that they don't work their way out.

2 Warped floorboards should be secured to the joists below with woodscrews. Nail loose boards down securely with new nails.

INSTALLING THE UNDERLAY

1 Unroll a length of underlay at right angles to the direction of the floorboards. Staple around the edges and at intervals across the middle. Cover the whole floor in this way, butting lengths together. Trim the ends of the underlay with a utility knife.

TIP

Laying hardboard
If your floorboards are very uneven it will not be possible to create a flat new floor without laying hardboard before you lay the cushioned underlay and the new flooring. Lay the panels smooth side up and secure each one with 3/4" (2 cm) finishing nails. Secure sheets 1/2" (1.3 cm) in from the edges, spacing the nails 6" (15 cm) apart. Space the nails at 9" (23 cm) intervals over the rest of the sheet. The time taken will be repaid in terms of extra comfort, and prolonged life of the new wood-strip. On a ground floor, the laying of hardboard also reduces heat loss through gaps between boards.

Shown below is the selection of finishes generally available at laminated wood-strip flooring suppliers. The surfaces are colored and grained to re-create the feel of the woods named.

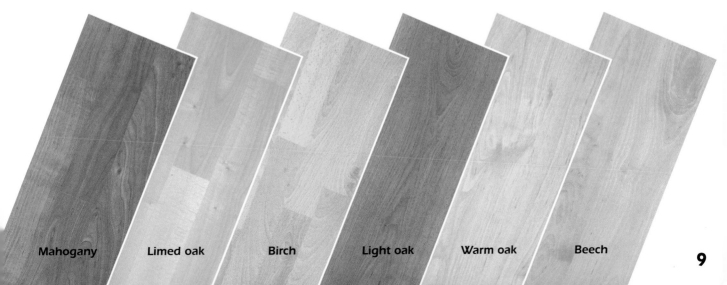

Mahogany   **Limed oak**   **Birch**   **Light oak**   **Warm oak**   **Beech**

LAYING THE FLOOR

1 Lay the first row of boards in place with their grooved edges next to the wall. Position some of the spacers against the baseboard and push the first board tight against them. Glue the narrow ends of the boards together. Cut the last board in the row to the correct length using a tenon saw or jigsaw.

2 Stagger lengthwise joints by using the offcut from the first row to start the next row. Apply glue to the grooved edge of this piece and slide it into place.

3 Place tamping block along edge of board. Tap groove into tongue of first row, using hammer. Wipe off excess glue quickly with damp cloth. Lay rows of boards across room.

4 Lay board for final row directly over the last full width board you have laid. Place a spare board on top of this, butting it against the spacers. Draw along the spare board's edge with a pencil to mark the cutting line on the middle board of the sandwich. Saw the board along the marked line.

5 Position the final board against the baseboard. Use a plank puller, shown here, or a small crowbar, to pull the joint together. Glue and fit the rest of the last row in the same way.

The immaculate appearance of the wood-strip floor in this glamorous bedroom is in sharp contrast to the romantic feel of the rest of the room. The sheer and luxuriant fluid lines of the fabrics add softness to the plain natural wood without overpowering the look of it and the whole effect is one of modern elegance.

DEALING WITH OBSTACLES

 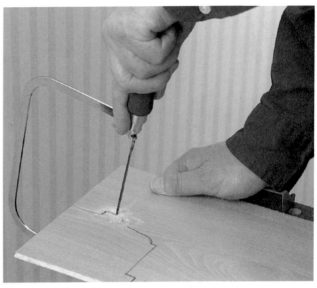

1 Press a profile gauge against the door frame to determine its shape. Trace around the shape on a board. If you don't have a profile gauge, slide a piece of paper underneath the door frame and draw around the shape of it. Transfer the shape to the board.

2 Cut out the shape of the door frame, using a coping saw (shown) or a fine-tooth blade on a jigsaw. Fine-tooth blades help prevent the wood-strip surface from chipping while it's being sawn.

3 Position the cut board in place to check that the fit is accurate. Sand cut edges as necessary. Measure and mark width of door frame on board, if necessary. Repeat steps 1 and 2; check accuracy of fit. Glue the board in place.

DEALING WITH RADIATOR PIPES

  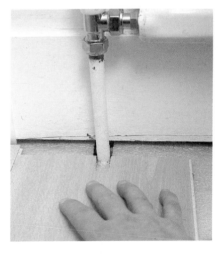

1 Butt the board up against the radiator pipe so that you can mark its position. Measure the distance from the side of the pipe to the wall and allow for the spacer. Drill a hole to match the pipe diameter.

2 Mark and carefully cut out the small segment that would be behind the pipe, trying not to damage the segment or lose it, as this will be needed later. Wipe off pencil mark with a damp cloth.

3 Slide the board in place. If you find that the gap between the pipe and the wall is small, cover it with molding. If it is large, replace the small cutout piece behind the pipe first, then cover with molding.

FINISHING OFF

1 Prepare the molding, marking 45° miter cuts to form the corners. Place a piece of scrap wood in the miter box first so you don't cut into the base of the box. Place the molding on top and saw the wood at the marks with the tenon saw.

2 Remove the spacers and secure the molding to the bottom of the baseboard with panel nails close to the corners and at 1 ft (30.5 cm) intervals. Don't nail it into the floor as the wood won't have room to expand and contract, which may result in boards buckling or separating.

Pergo laminate flooring

Floor Care

● Heavy furniture can leave permanent dents in the surface of your floor so invest in rubber cups to put under the legs of sofas and armchairs and bed castors. Don't drag furniture across the floor; lift it wherever possible to avoid scuff marks.

● Use rugs or mats to protect the floor in areas that are in constant use or that are susceptible to spills.

● Wipe up spills immediately and try to protect the floor from damp (never place a potted plant on the floor without a tray, for example). Liquid that seeps into the floor can cause the boards to warp and stain.

● Discourage the wearing of high-heeled shoes on the floor as these will cause dents. Also black-soled shoes and rubber-soled shoes can leave marks that are hard to remove.

◀ *A rug not only offers comfort, color and textural contrast, but protects the areas of maximum use in a room, such as the sofa area in this den. The space between the sofas and coffee table would be particularly susceptible to scuffs and spills.*

WOOD MOLDING FRAMES

Add architectural detail to a room by adding wood molding on plain walls or featureless surfaces such as modern flush doors and bath surrounds.

You can use decorative moldings to frame features such as a picture or mirror, or assemble pairs and groups of frames to give the look of period molding or simply add interest to a flat surface. Moldings are available in a variety of decorative profiles from home improvement centers and lumberyards. They are sold by the foot or in kit form.

Self-adhesive kits are quick and easy to install but, because they are designed for detailing doors, they are only available in a limited range of sizes and shapes. For larger projects, you can cut the molding yourself using a miter box, then secure it in place with finishing nails and wood glue.

To help work out the best size and arrangement of frames, hang strips of paper in a frame shape to judge the effect. Molding frames often match the size of other architectural details in a room, such as the width of the windows or fireplace. With a series of frames – along a dado for example – they don't all have to be the same size but they are usually symmetrical.

▶ *A row of wood frames spaced evenly along a wall transforms a plain dado. A subtle, dragged paint effect on both wall and frames unifies the look.*

ATTACHING A PANEL KIT

Using a self-adhesive kit is the simplest way to add wood panel moldings – you simply peel off the backing and press them into place. Since they are difficult to remove once in place, it's important to measure accurately and position the panels carefully.

Although you can use panel kits on various surfaces, they are designed for doors, so they come in a variety of sizes for standard door widths. If using on a door, check the packaging for recommended spacing.

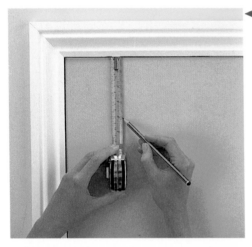

◄**1** Apply your preferred finish – paint, stain or varnish – to the molding. Take care to keep the finish well away from the adhesive backing strip.

2 Prepare the door or other surface and apply your finish to it, if desired. Allow to dry. Alternatively, clean the surface with a mild detergent to remove any grease. Allow to dry. Make sure the surface is dust free.

◄**3** Use a steel tape measure and pencil to mark the position of the panel moldings on the surface; if attaching panels to a door, check the kit instructions for positioning. Use a carpenter's level to make sure the markings are square.

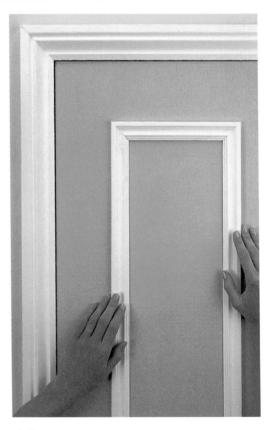

5 Align the panel with the pencil marks on the surface. Press lightly at one or two places to hold it in place. When satisfied that it is in the correct position, press firmly along all four sides.

4 Place the panel facedown on a clean surface. Starting at the corners, carefully peel off the backing strips to expose the adhesive layer.

CUTTING YOUR OWN PANEL MOLDINGS

Attaching the panel molding

It's straightforward to make panels of any size if you use a miter box to help cut the moldings at neat 45° angles. For speedy results, you can use double-sided adhesive tape or a hot glue gun to attach the moldings. For a more secure attachment on a wall, use finishing nails hammered into the wall studs. On hollow walls, locate the wall studs by knocking on the wall and listening for a less hollow sound – they are usually spaced 16" (40.5 cm) apart.

1 Cut paper strips the same width as the molding. Hang the strips on the wall with poster putty, in a panel shape. Experiment with the size and shape of the paper panel until you are pleased with the effect. Use a carpenter's level and framing square to check that the strips are level and square. Mark the outer edges of the paper.

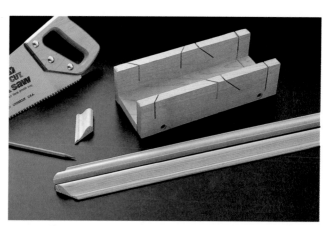

2 Measure the length of the upper paper strip and mark this length on the wooden molding. Use a miter box and tenon saw to cut both ends of the molding, angling the cuts in from the marks. Cut the lower piece of molding to match, then measure and cut molding for the panel sides.

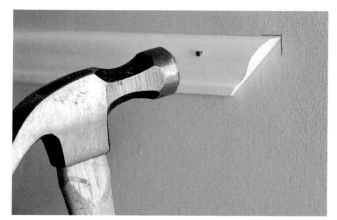

3 Seal any knots with shellac or stain killer and finish as desired. Drill holes 1" (2.5 cm) from the ends of the molding and, if necessary, at intervals between, to coincide with the wall studs. Hammer nails partway through the holes. Apply wood glue to the back of the upper molding and hammer it into position, leaving the nail heads slightly raised.

4 Position the side molding strips and hammer in only the top nail. Attach the lower molding strip, using a framing square to ensure that the panel is square. Secure the remaining nails in the side strips.

5 Countersink the nails, using a hammer and nail set. Touch up the nail holes with paint or filler.

▼ *Make a special feature of a favorite picture by surrounding it with pre-assembled paneling. Here, a different wallcovering pattern is used inside the panel frame to emphasize the paneling.*

▲ *A single rectangular panel molding adds elegant solidity and a period feel to an exterior door. The molding has been cut to match the width of the glazed area of the door and blends perfectly with the existing style of the door.*

◄ *Modern flush doors benefit from the period look of panel moldings, even in a contemporary setting. Simple to secure with self-adhesive tape, this Georgian-style panel kit has been used with obvious success.*

ALCOVE CUPBOARD

Make the most of all your available room by building a smart cupboard to fit neatly in an alcove. You can make the cupboard any size to suit the dimensions of your room.

Building your own alcove cupboard, rather than using a ready-made version, enables you to make it fit the dimensions of your alcove perfectly, with no unsightly gaps at the sides. The cupboard featured here is made from two cupboard doors attached to a medium-density fiberboard (MDF) panel that has been cut to fit across the front of the alcove. The top of the cupboard and the shelf inside are also cut from MDF. When building the cupboard, mounting strips are cut to length and secured to the alcove walls to support the shelf and top and to secure the front panel firmly in place.

You can either build the cupboard to fit flush with the walls on each side of the alcove, or let it extend slightly beyond the alcove to give even more storage space. Instructions for both styles are given on the following pages. If your room has baseboard running around it, you will need to cut contours in the lower edges of some of the MDF pieces to ensure a perfect fit.

Buy the cupboard doors first and make sure they are a suitable size and proportion for your alcove, allowing a good border all around to frame the doors and support the hinges and catches. You can buy cupboard doors in a variety of sizes and styles from most home improvement centers. Once you've determined exact measurements for your cupboard, you may take them to a full-service lumberyard where the MDF can be cut for you. The holes behind the doors are cut using a jigsaw.

▲ *For a harmonious finish, paint your alcove cupboard to coordinate with the surrounding room scheme. Here, the cupboard has been painted in soft pastel shades to complement the light and airy feel of a soft modern decor.*

Making an Alcove Cupboard

You will need

- Two cupboard doors
- Medium-density fiberboard (MDF), ¾" (2 cm) thick
- Mounting strip lumber, 1" x 2" (2.5 x 5 cm)
- Metal ruler and pencil
- Drill and drill bits, and ⅛" countersink bit
- Jigsaw

- Sandpaper, medium grade
- Primer and paintbrush
- Carpenter's level
- Countersink woodscrews, 1" (2.5 cm)
- Masonry drill bit for brick walls and/or drill bit for hollow walls to match anchors and molly bolts
- Plastic anchors or molly bolts

- Screwdriver
- Finishing nails, 1" (2.5 cm)
- Hammer
- Nail set
- Wood filler
- Cupboard door hinges and screws to match
- Paint in your chosen color and finish
- Cupboard door knobs and catches

Measuring and cutting out

Front panel Measure the width of the alcove. Cut a piece of MDF to this width, by the height of the cupboard doors, plus 4¾" (12 cm) or as desired. If the cupboard is to be flush with the alcove, cut a small section out of each lower corner to fit around the baseboard at each side. If the cupboard is to extend beyond the alcove, just cut out the section from the corner that will sit against the baseboard.

Top panel Measure the depth of the cupboard: this will be either equal to the depth of the alcove, or slightly deeper if the cupboard is to extend beyond the alcove. Cut a piece of MDF the width of the alcove by the desired depth of the cupboard, plus ⅜" (1 cm) to create a slight overhang.

Mounting strips Cut four mounting strips the width of the alcove. For a cupboard that will lie flush with the alcove, cut four lengths of mounting strip to the alcove depth, minus 1⁵⁄₁₆" (3.3 cm) to allow for the width of MDF and back strips. For a cupboard that will extend beyond the alcove, cut two strips to the desired depth of the cupboard minus 1⁵⁄₁₆" (3.3 cm); and two strips to the depth of the alcove minus 5" (12.5 cm), to allow for back

strip and for the side extension panel to be slotted in.

Side extension piece (optional) Cut a piece of MDF to the height of the cupboard doors plus 4¾" (12 cm), by the desired extension beyond the alcove plus 4" (10 cm). Cut a section from the lower back corner to fit it over the baseboard.

Shelf Cut a piece of MDF the width of the alcove by the desired cupboard depth minus ¾" (2 cm). If the cupboard is to extend beyond the alcove, cut a section from one front corner of the shelf to accommodate the side extension piece.

Alcove cupboard components

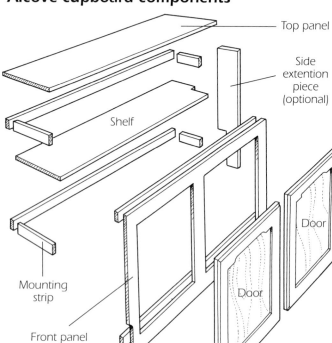

Top panel

Side extension piece (optional)

Shelf

Door

Door

Mounting strip

Front panel

1 Sand smooth the cut edges on all the pieces. Draw a line down the center of the front panel, from one long edge to the other. Lay the two doors on the front panel, one on each side of the marked line, at least ¾" (2 cm) from it; position them so that they are centered across the width of each half, with the border above each slightly smaller than the one below.

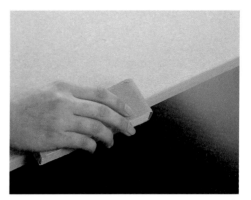

2 Check the doors are square to the panel edges, then draw around them with a pencil. Remove the doors. Draw a smaller square inside each marked square, 3/8" (1 cm) from the edge.

3 Drill a hole, large enough to take the jigsaw blade, in each corner of the smaller marked squares. Saw along the inner marked lines to cut out both panels. Sand the cut edges smooth.

4 Sand one long front edge of the cupboard top panel, to round it and give a smooth, professional finish. Mark the positions for the mounting strips on the back and side walls of the alcove. For the top strips, mark a line the height of the cupboard front panel along the wall, using a pencil and carpenter's level. Repeat to mark the positions for the shelf strips.

5 Predrill screw holes, using countersink bit, along the wider face of the short mounting strips and two long strips; position holes 2" (5 cm) from each end of the short strips and 5" (12.5 cm) from each end of the long strips. Add a third hole 1" (2.5 cm) off center of each long strip.

◄ *6* Position the wider face of one long strip against the back wall, with the top edge level with the marked line for the shelf; mark the positions of the screw holes on the wall. Remove the strip and predrill screw holes in the wall. Insert plastic wall anchors (brick walls) or molly bolts (hollow walls) into the drilled holes. Reposition the back shelf strip on the wall, with the countersunk side out and the screw holes aligned; drive in the screws. Repeat for the side strips for the shelf and for the back and side top strips that will support the top of the cupboard.

▲ *You can paint the inside of the cupboard to coordinate or contrast with the color scheme of the room. For a subtle, integrated finish, the inside back and side walls of this cupboard were simply left the same color as the surrounding walls of the room, with the shelf, baseboard and all the mounting strips painted to match.*

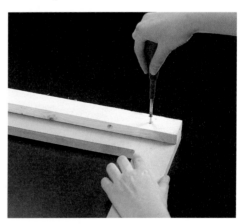

7 Predrill screw holes, using the countersink bit on the two remaining mounting strips: on the wider face, position them 2" (5 cm) from each end, plus an extra hole 1" (2.5 cm) off center; on the narrower face, position them 5" (12.5 cm) from each end, plus one in the center. Lay the wider face of the strips on the wrong side of the front panel as shown, countersunk side up; position one flush with the top edge and the other flush with the bottom edge. Screw in place. The holes on the narrow face will enable you to secure the front piece to the floor and cupboard top. Prime all the cupboard sections.

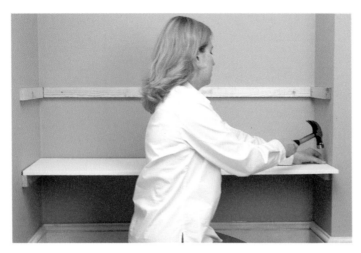

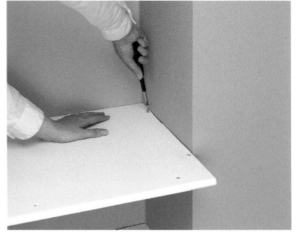

8 Predrill nail holes ½" (1.3 cm) from each short edge and 3" (7.5 cm) from each long edge of the shelf; for an extended cupboard, predrill the hole 3" (7.5 cm) from the edge of the cutout section of the shelf. Place the shelf on the mounting strips and hammer finishing nails through the drilled holes. Countersink the nails using a nail set.

9 Predrill screw holes, using countersink bit, on the top piece: ½" (1.3 cm) in from the back and side edges and ⅞" (2.2 cm) in from the front edge; position them about 1" (2.5 cm) from each corner of the back and side edges, plus one at the center of the back edge. Make sure the holes on the front edge match the corresponding holes on the front mounting strip. Position the top piece on the upper mounting strips, and screw it in place.

10 Proceed ➤ to step 11 if your cupboard design is flush with the alcove walls. Slip the side extension piece in place and predrill screw holes, using countersink bit, to match the center of the shelf edge (for a long extension, predrill two parallel holes at the shelf). Screw the side piece to the side edge of the shelf and to the top piece.

11 Position the front of the cupboard. Use a carpenter's level ➤ to check that it is perfectly straight. Screw the bottom mounting strip securely to the floor through the predrilled holes. Screw the cupboard top to the strip at the top of the front, screwing down through the predrilled holes in the top.

◄*12* Fill the countersunk holes with filler, allow to dry, then sand smooth. Mark the positions for the hinges on the outside edge of each door and on the cupboard front, by tracing the screw holes in the hinge; use the original pencil lines around the holes cut in the front of the cupboard as a guide for positioning. Screw the hinges to the door edge first, then to the cupboard front.

13 Apply two coats of paint, allowing it to dry and sanding smooth between coats, if necessary. Attach handles to the front of the doors, and catches to the inside edge of each door and beneath the shelf at the corresponding point.

RADIATOR COVER

A free-standing radiator cabinet is an effective way of integrating a radiator into a room scheme. This neat and elegant unit is simple to make using pre-cut MDF and softwood.

Radiators are a typical feature of older homes but they can be visually intrusive. The most effective way to camouflage a radiator is to conceal it behind a custom-made cabinet. This is a particularly good solution in period-style rooms, where you can build the cover to match architectural details. A radiator cover also provides useful shelf space – a place to leave keys or mail in a hallway, for example.

Ready-made cabinets are available from several suppliers, but you can make your own at a fraction of the cost. The cabinet featured here is constructed from medium-density fiberboard (MDF). Full-service lumberyards will cut the board to size if you provide them with exact measurements.

The directions assume that the radiator is set just above the baseboard. The baseboard on the radiator cover is the same height as the wall baseboard – to visually integrate the radiator cover into the room scheme. If you can miter baseboard freehand (it is too deep for standard miter boxes), select a length that matches the existing board in height and design. Otherwise, combine a lumber strip with a suitable molding. For example, the cover featured here has a baseboard made from 1" x 4" (2.5 x 10 cm) lumber topped with 2½" (6.5 cm) molding, to match a 6" (15 cm) baseboard.

If your radiator has a thermostatic valve, make sure the valve remains on the outside of your finished cover, so that the air continues to circulate around it freely.

▲ *A made-to-measure cabinet is an effective way of concealing an unattractive radiator. Here, the cabinet has been painted to blend with the decorative scheme of the hallway; simply prime, sand and then finish with two coats of low-luster paint for a perfect, durable finish.*

Assembling the Radiator Cover

YOU WILL NEED

- Medium-density fiberboard (MDF), ¾" (2 cm) thick
- Decorative molding for shelf
- Ornamental hardboard grille
- Lumber, 1" x 4" (2.5 x 10 cm), and molding for baseboard
- Steel tape measure
- Fine-tooth saw and miter box
- Wood glue; weights
- Finishing nails, 1¼" (3.2 cm), and hammer
- Sandpaper, fine grade
- Latex primer and paint

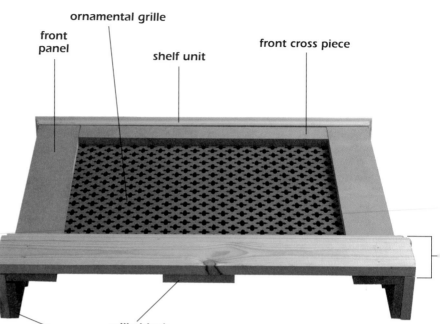

ornamental grille
front panel
shelf unit
front cross piece
side panel
grille block
baseboard made of strip lumber and molding

Measuring and cutting out

Measure as in step 1, then cut the following:

From MDF:

2 side panels Height: floor to top of radiator plus 2" (5 cm); depth: wall to front of radiator plus 1⅜" (3.5 cm).

2 front panels Height: floor to top of radiator plus 2" (5 cm); width: 4" (10 cm).

Front cross piece Width: width of radiator; depth: 3" (7.5 cm).

Top shelf Width: width of radiator plus 8" (20.5 cm); depth: depth of side panel plus 1 1/16" (1.8 cm).

Grille block Height: same as radiator baseboard; width: 6" (15 cm).

Decorative molding, baseboard, grille Cut according to the size of the assembled MDF frame (see steps 4-10).

1 Take the following measurements: the distance from the floor to the top of the radiator; the width of the radiator; the distance from the wall to the front of the radiator. Prepare a cutting list based on the specifications in **Measuring and cutting out**, left.

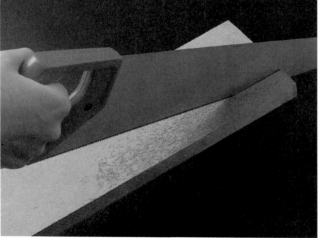

2 Hold the side panels up to the baseboard. Mark the height and depth of the baseboard. Use saw to cut a notch in each side panel to allow it to fit over the baseboard.

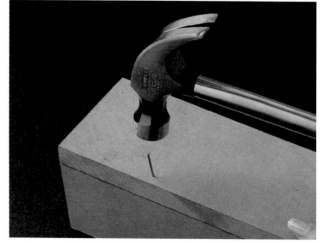

3 Butt, glue and nail the two front panels to the edge of the side panels as shown. Allow to dry for the recommended time.

4 Miter one end of the decorative molding for the shelf, using saw and miter box. Hold it up to the front edge of the shelf, with the miter against one corner. Mark the location of the second corner in pencil – to avoid mistakes, mark the direction of the miter cut. Cut the miter. Measure, mark and cut the side pieces in the same way – they will be mitered at one end only. Glue and nail the molding to the front and sides of the shelf. Allow to dry.

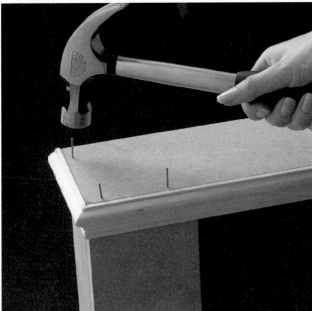

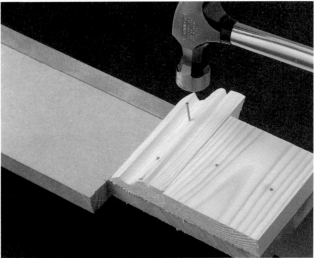

5 Stand the two side units on the floor. Glue and nail the shelf unit on top of the side units.

6 Position the baseboard strip lumber across side unit and mark a cutting line; cut, glue and nail the length in place. Position the baseboard molding across the top of baseboard strip, mark the correct lengths and cut miter. Glue and nail in place. Repeat on other side.

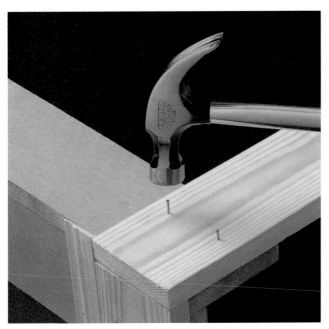

7 Hold baseboard strip to the front of the unit to form a butt joint, and mark the cutting line. Cut it to length, glue and nail the piece to the front.

8 Miter one end of the remaining baseboard molding, hold it in position across the top of the baseboard strip and mark the location of the other corner in pencil, noting the direction of the miter cut. Cut the second miter. Glue and nail the molding in place. Allow to dry.

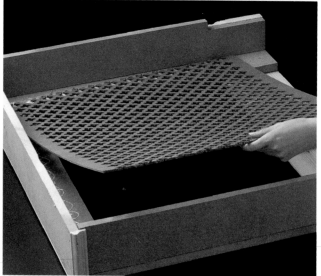

$\mathcal{9}$ Turn the unit over. Glue the front cross piece to the back of the shelf molding and the sides of the front panels. Glue and nail the grille block to the center back of the baseboard. Cut the ornamental grille to the width of the radiator plus 6⅜" (16 cm), using saw. Ensure that the panel is symmetrical by centering the grille motif on the front of the cover. Apply glue to the backs of the front cross piece, the side panels and the grille block.

$\mathcal{10}$ Lay the ornamental grille in place and secure it at intervals around the edges, using nails. Apply weights to the glued points – extra pressure improves the bond and accelerates the drying time. When the cover is completely dry, prime it and paint it the color of your choice.

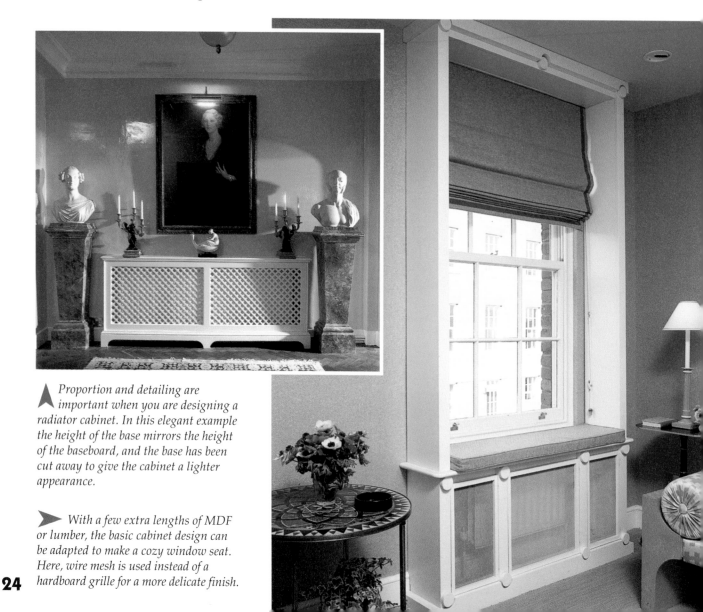

▲ *Proportion and detailing are important when you are designing a radiator cabinet. In this elegant example the height of the base mirrors the height of the baseboard, and the base has been cut away to give the cabinet a lighter appearance.*

▶ *With a few extra lengths of MDF or lumber, the basic cabinet design can be adapted to make a cozy window seat. Here, wire mesh is used instead of a hardboard grille for a more delicate finish.*

COVERED CORNICES

*Make your own wooden cornice and cover it with a
wallcovering border for a professional finish. Paint the edges
to match or coordinate with the edge of the border.*

A wooden cornice is straightforward to make, requiring very few skills. It provides an easy alternative to a fabric valance and, teamed with sheer curtain panels or a simple roller shade or blind, it forms a pleasing option for windows. A cornice also disguises hardware at the top of a window. The wooden cornice made on the following pages is painted along the edges and covered with a coordinating wallcovering border for a sleek, tailored finish.

You can create a variety of different looks that will suit many room styles. Choose a wallcovering border that is wide enough to cover the whole of the completed cornice. Alternatively, make a cornice with a shaped lower edge and use a narrower border to partially cover the cornice. Whether you choose a straight or shaped edge, make sure that the completed cornice is deep enough to cover any blind or curtain heading and its hardware.

▲ *A brightly colored wallcovering
border decorated with bowls of
fruit adds a jaunty, tropical air to a
kitchen or dining room.*

How to Make a Covered Box Cornice

YOU WILL NEED

- ½" (1.3 cm) plywood
- Saw
- Wood glue
- Wood filler
- 1" (2.5 cm) finishing nails
- Hammer
- Nail set
- Sandpaper, fine grade
- Primer

- Paint
- Wallcovering border
- Scissors
- Wallcovering adhesive
- Sponge applicator
- Pencil
- Power drill; drill bits
- Woodscrews, molly bolts, angle irons and screwdriver (optional)
- Carpenter's level

Cutting instructions

Determine the inside measurement for the cornice once the blind or curtains are in place. The cornice should clear the front of the window treatment by 2" to 3" (5 to 7.5 cm), and extend at least 2" (5 cm) beyond either side of the window.

Cornice top Measure and cut the plywood to correspond to the inside measurements of the cornice, as determined above.

Cornice front Cut to the height of the wallcovering border by the length of the cornice top, plus twice the thickness of the plywood.

Cornice sides Cut to the height of the border by the depth of the cornice top.

1 Apply wood glue to the short edges of the cornice top. Attach each side piece to the top piece, aligning the upper edges. Attach the front piece in the same way, aligning it with the top and side pieces. Secure along the edges with finishing nails.

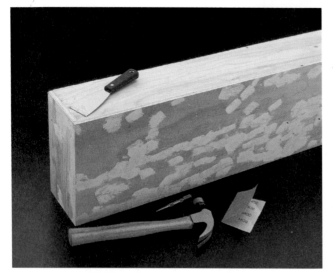

2 Set the nails, using nail set and hammer. Fill the nail holes, the edges of the plywood and any uneven surfaces with wood filler. Smooth the front and side surfaces and edges with fine-grade sandpaper.

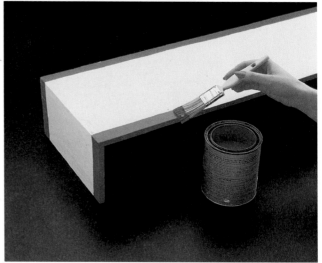

3 Apply the primer; allow to dry. Paint the lower edges and top of the cornice, extending the paint slightly over the edges to the front and sides; paint the inside of the cornice.

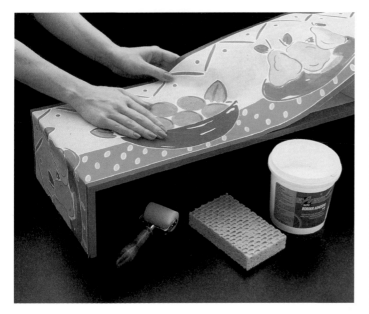

4 Cut a length of wallcovering border equal to the distance around the sides and front of the cornice plus 4" (10 cm). Mix the adhesive and apply it to the border. Center the border on the cornice, and working outward, smooth the border over the front and sides, taking care not to trap air bubbles. Wrap the border over the back edge of the cornice and allow to dry. Trim off the excess paper.

5 Hook the cornice over the window frame and drive finishing nails down into the frame. Or, secure angle irons to the wall to align with inner ends of cornice and at 40" (102 cm) intervals, if necessary; drill into wall studs or use molly bolts. Attach cornice to angle irons.

Shaped-edge cornices

Create more interesting effects using cornices with shaped lower edges. Make the cornices in exactly the same way as for the plain cornice, but allow for the shaped lower edge when considering which wallcovering border to use; the border must be narrow enough to fit above the shaped edge. If you use a very narrow border, you can position it between the top of the cornice and the top of the patterned area, if desired. Finish the top edge and emphasize the lower shaped edge by painting them in a color that matches or contrasts with the border.

Use a stylized leaf border with a gold painted edge to create an exotic cornice.

Add a cottage garden border with a coordinating edge for a country look.

For a classic look, use a large floral print border and a harmonious pastel shade for the lower edge.

Vinyl adhesive borders

Vinyl adhesive borders are now available and they take the hard work and mess out of applying borders. You simply remove the paper backing from the wrong side of the border and smooth it over the surface of the cornice. The borders bond quickly and are difficult to remove once attached, so work slowly, inch by inch, to achieve a smooth, accurate finish.

➤ *Create a bright, modern look with a bold checked wallcovering border and zigzag-edged cornice. The edge of the cornice has been painted yellow to match both the border and the window drapes.*

▲ *The wallcovering border used on this straight-edged cornice makes a perfect choice for a child's room. The colorful multi-striped edging provides an attractive alternative finish.*

➤ *A delicate fretwork design and pretty floral border create a look that's perfect for a bedroom. The pastel shades on the border blend perfectly with the painted lower edge of the cornice.*

PANEL-EFFECT WINDOW SHUTTERS

These internal window shutters, with their attractive detailing, are simple to make using just two sheets of MDF and decorative wood molding.

Window shutters provide insulation in the winter months, help keep the home cool in the summer heat, and offer extra security, particularly for vulnerable ground floor or basement windows. Traditionally, shutters were constructed as an integral part of the window structure, folding in from the side to cover the window. These simple shutters, which fold back flat against the wall on either side of the window, are easy to install in today's homes, and fulfill a decorative and functional role.

Similar to doors in their construction, classic softwood shutters are made using a complex series of joints. The shutters featured here have been designed to emulate the paneled, jointed look, but are built very simply with few tools and minimum woodworking skills. They are made from two sheets of MDF, one cut, one plain, which are sandwiched together to create a paneled effect. The panels are enhanced with decorative molding, chosen to match the depth of the MDF for a flush fit.

The finished shutters are hinged to lengths of mounting strip before installation, to make the final hanging easy.

For additional security, you can 'panel' both sides of the shutters by attaching a third sheet of MDF, following the instructions in steps 1 to 6, to the plain side.

▲ *Panel-effect window shutters provide a highly decorative window treatment, and make an attractive – and practical – substitute for curtains or blinds.*

MAKING WINDOW SHUTTERS

- MDF, ¼" and ⅜" (6 mm and 1 cm) thick
- Pencil, ruler
- Drill, large and small drill bits, countersink bit, masonry bit
- Jigsaw
- Sandpaper, medium grade
- Wood glue
- C-clamps, scrap wood
- Tape measure
- Miter box

- Tenon saw
- Decorative hinges
- Awl
- Screwdrivers, medium and small
- 1" x 2" (2.5 x 5 cm) lumber strip
- Countersink screws
- Latex primer and paint
- Wall anchors
- Shutter fittings

Measuring and cutting out

For the shutters

Measure the height and width of your window, allowing an extra inch (2.5 cm) all around. Halve the width measurement to give you the final shutter size. Cut four rectangles to this size: two from the ¼" (6 mm) MDF and two from the ⅜" (1 cm) MDF. Sand the edges.

For the mounting strip

Cut lumber strip to same length as shutter height.

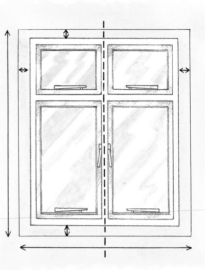

MAKING THE PANELED SECTIONS

1 Draw a line 2¼" (6 cm) from the top, bottom and sides of the two ⅜" (1 cm) MDF boards, to create a border. Measure, mark and draw a 2¼" (6 cm) bar across the center of each section. This will give you your panel outlines. Use a jigsaw to cut out the center of each panel, drilling out the corners as on page 17, step 3.

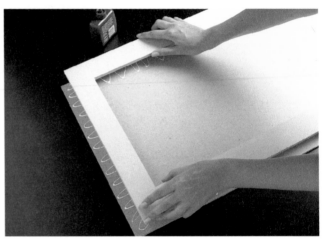

2 Align edges of cut front board with a plain back board; trace 'panel' openings. Apply wood glue to the first back board, then place front board on top. Work quickly, while the glue is still wet, and align the edges of the two pieces until you have a perfect match.

3 Clamp the sections together with C-clamps, using short lengths of scrap wood to prevent indentations or marks. Set aside to dry. Repeat the gluing and clamping process to create the second shutter.

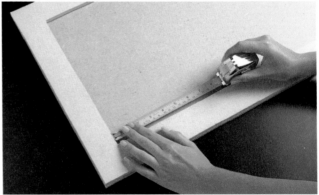

4 Measure each inside edge of each panel with a tape measure, and note the measurements. (To ensure that the molding fits perfectly, it's important to measure each length individually, since fractional changes can alter the precision of your miters.)

5 Miter the decorative molding to the correct length, using a tenon saw and miter box. Work one panel at a time and check the fit as you go.

6 Apply wood glue to the panel and molding. Position each molding piece, pressing down firmly as you work for a perfect fit; wipe off excess glue.

FINISHING AND HANGING THE SHUTTERS

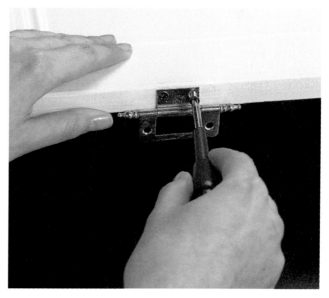

1 Undercoat each shutter, painting both the paneled and the plain side in quick succession to prevent warping, which happens when the drying process of the paint causes the surface of the MDF to shrink slightly. When dry, paint the shutters in the color of your choice, sanding between coats, if necessary.

2 Mark the position of the hinges through the screw holes with an awl. Drill pilot holes for each screw; screw hinges in place.

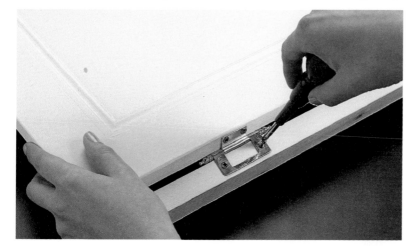

3 Align each length of mounting strip with the shutter sides, checking that they are level top and bottom. Mark all hinge positions on the mounting strip with the awl, drill pilot holes and screw in place. Hold both shutters in the closed position against the window, and draw a pencil line or series of marks down the wall along the mounting strip to mark its position. Unscrew both sections of mounting strip.

4 Drill three or four pilot holes in each molding strip using a countersink bit. Hold one strip against the wall along the marked line, and mark through each hole with an awl. Set aside the strip; drill holes in the wall at each marked point. Insert wall anchors.

▲ Here, the shutters have been hung with the paneled side opening out against the wall. They provide an attractive frame for an otherwise plain window, in addition to offering extra security and insulation when closed.

5 Screw the strip lengths back onto the shutter hinges, then with a friend to help you support the shutters at the window, screw the whole assembly to the wall. Add any shutter hardware such as holdbacks or clasps or bolts.

▶ The plain side of the shutters has a painted faux paneled effect. To create this look, mask the 'paneled' areas with masking tape, and paint, using a stronger and a darker shade of your finished shutter color.

WOODEN TRUNK MAKEOVER

Transform an old wooden trunk into a chest to treasure
using simple decoupage techniques, hand-painted motifs
in bright acrylics and a touch of metallic wax.

The art of decoupage is a quick and easy way to give an old piece of furniture an exciting new look. A damaged surface is easily disguised and strengthened with layered papers. On the trunk featured here, brightly colored hand-made papers are used to give an exotic Mexican look, and the surface is further embellished with simple hand-painted shapes and motifs in vivid acrylic paints. Finally, a decorative raised effect is added around the decoupaged shapes, using a gold relief liner.

If you don't have an old trunk, take a look around local second-hand shops where you can often pick up bargains. Alternatively, adapt the directions to give a new look to a smaller-scale wooden storage box.

Before you begin decorating the trunk, decide on a basic color scheme or theme, such as the Mexican look featured here. You'll find a wide range of handmade papers to inspire you at art supply stores, or you can use gift wrap or leftover wallpaper. Dimensional paints are available in a range of colors at arts and crafts stores.

▼ *Handmade papers in bright red, green, blue, yellow and orange have been used to give this trunk a cheerful new look. Simple shapes and motifs, hand-painted in colorful acrylics and gold dimensional paint, add to the Mexican tapestry.*

DECORATING THE TRUNK

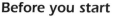

- Trunk
- Wire brush or scraper
- Sandpaper, coarse and medium grades
- Cloth and mild detergent
- Paintbrush
- Acrylic paint, in raw umber and a range of decorative colors, such as white, orange, dark blue and light blue
- Handmade paper in bright colors, such as red, green, blue, yellow and orange
- Scissors
- Decoupage medium
- Utility knife
- Artist's brush
- Dimensional paint liner
- Metallic wax, soft cloth

Before you start

Examine the trunk before you begin decorating it, to see if it needs any basic repairs. Glue, clamp and nail or screw weak joints. Replace damaged hinges and locks. Clean tin with diluted vinegar. Remove rust using fine steel wool and lubricant oil; wipe with mineral spirits to remove oil residue.

1 Remove any flaking paint and loose material, using a wire brush or scraper. Smooth away any awkward bumps with sandpaper, using a coarse grade first, then a medium grade. Wipe the surfaces with a soapy cloth to remove any grease or dust; rinse with a clean damp cloth. Allow to dry thoroughly.

2 Apply a coat of raw umber acrylic paint to any raised bars or struts across the top or on the sides of the trunk; allow the paint to dry thoroughly. Apply a second coat of paint to the same areas, if necessary.

3 Cut handmade paper (red and green are used here), slightly larger than the top and sides of your trunk. If the trunk has raised bars, struts or separate panels across the top or sides, cut the paper in strips and alternate colors for a really bright look. Apply a generous coat of decoupage medium to the area of the trunk to be covered. Smooth the paper in place with your fingers, working from the center to the edges and removing air pockets as you go.

4 Trim the paper to fit within the trunk edges, using the tip of a sharp utility knife. If your trunk has large bolts or raised tacks across the top or sides, cut a small cross in the paper covering them; gently peel away the paper from the center of the cross, then trim neatly around the edge of the bolt or tack with the knife. Apply and trim paper to each area to be covered.

5 Cut small squares of contrasting papers to apply over the paper strips on the trunk top and sides. Lay the paper squares, evenly spaced, along each strip of paper, and secure with decoupage medium. Cut small strips of paper to frame each square, selecting a different color than both the background strip and the square. Apply the strips around each square, using decoupage medium. Allow to dry, then apply a final coat of decoupage medium over all the papers. Allow to dry.

6 Paint simple shapes such as crosses, small squares and circles at the center of each framed paper square, using an artist's brush and acrylic paints in two or three contrasting colors. Allow to dry thoroughly.

7 Paint a thin line around some of the painted shapes to define the outline. Avoid smudging the lines of previously painted motifs as you work across the trunk. Allow to dry.

8 Add further details to each decorated paper square, using a dimensional paint liner: draw tiny crosses, circles and wavy lines onto the painted motifs and around each square.

9 Rub a little metallic wax along the edges of the wood struts or bars, using your fingertips. Buff the wax to a soft sheen, using a soft cloth.

▲ *Create the appearance of patchwork on a small storage chest, by decoupaging it with a multitude of colorful textured papers, torn into shapes and laid onto the surface to overlap one another. A silver dimensional paint is applied over the edges to give the impression of stitching.*

KITCHEN CHAIR MAKEOVER

*With a few basic repairs, some colorful paintwork
and three or four cutout motifs, you can give
a neglected kitchen chair a glorious new look.*

Most people have a battered old kitchen chair lying around the house, either forgotten in the attic or abandoned in the corner of a spare room. It takes very little time, effort and expense to transform it into a striking showpiece – like the chairs shown below and on the following pages, which are decorated following a folk-art theme.

Before you begin painting your chair, check it over to see what basic repairs (if any) need to be made. The chair might simply need washing down and sanding, or you might need to treat it for woodworm or replace missing struts. Next decide on the paint colors – you can copy the colors used here, or choose alternatives that are more suited to your room scheme. Simple folk-art shapes, such as flowers and hearts, work best for the wooden motifs and are easy to cut out.

A chair painted sunflower yellow with a sky-blue seat is a cheerful addition to this rustic kitchen. Simple flower shapes cut from thin wood add a folksy finish to the chair back.

CREATING A FOLK-ART CHAIR

YOU WILL NEED

- ➤ Wooden chair
- ➤ Sandpaper, medium grade
- ➤ Soft cloth
- ➤ Woodworm treatment (optional)
- ➤ Wood filler (optional)
- ➤ Length of dowel
- ➤ Wood glue

- ➤ Twine and small piece of wood
- ➤ Latex paint, in two or more colors
- ➤ Paintbrush
- ➤ Metallic wax in dark and light tones
- ➤ Clear acrylic sealer

- ➤ Thin card
- ➤ Pencil and scissors
- ➤ Balsa wood, 1/16" (1.5 mm) thick, about 4" x 16" (10 x 40.5 cm)
- ➤ 4 small tacks
- ➤ Needlenose pliers
- ➤ Hammer

PREPARING THE CHAIR

Before you start

Before painting and decorating your chair, it's essential to make all necessary repairs, and to prepare the surface for painting. The chair shown here was thoroughly sanded, treated for woodworm, and missing struts were replaced (see steps 1-3 for details). It's important to treat woodworm before bringing the chair into your home.

1 Use medium-grade sandpaper to sand all the surfaces of the chair. Remove any dust with a soft cloth.

2 Spray a woodworm treatment into the holes if the chair has signs of woodworm, and allow to dry. Once treated, the holes can be left as they are. Or fill them for a more uniform effect, using wood filler; smooth with sandpaper when dry.

3 Replace a missing or broken strut by cutting a length of dowel to match the existing struts and glue it into the holes. Hold it firmly in place while the glue dries by tying one leg to the other. Insert a small piece of wood between the strings to act as a lever; twist the wood to tighten the strings and hook it over the strut. Allow glue to dry.

DECORATING THE CHAIR

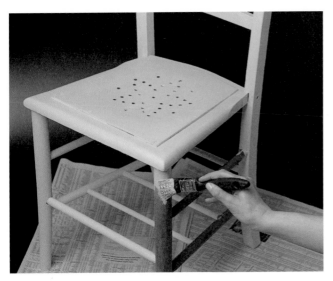

1 Paint the chair with two coats of latex paint, and allow to dry.

2 Paint the seat of the chair with two coats of contrasting paint. Allow to dry.

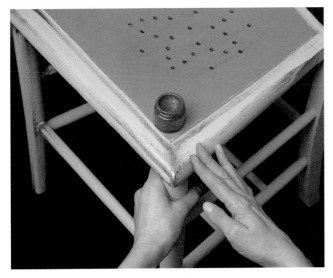

3 Rub dark metallic wax around the edges, legs and struts of the chair. Use the wax sparingly; gradually build up the color on edges and prominent details, for an appearance of natural wear.

4 Highlight areas with the light metallic wax, applying it sparingly over the dark wax. The holes in the seat of the chair shown here were highlighted by carefully working the wax around each edge.

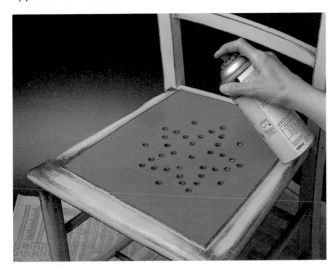

5 Apply two coats of clear acrylic sealer to the chair, allowing it to dry between coats. Allow to dry.

6 Draw and cut out a simple motif template, using card. Draw around the template onto balsa wood several times. Cut out the shapes and lightly sand the edges smooth.

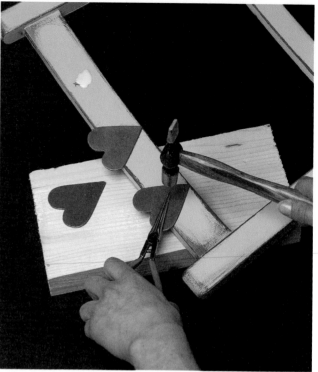

7 Color both sides of each motif using the dark metallic wax. Highlight the motif edges with the light wax. Finish with a coat of acrylic sealer.

8 Mark the points where the motifs will lie on the back of the chair, and squeeze a small blob of wood glue at each marked point. Secure the motifs in place using single tacks, holding the tacks upright with needlenose pliers. Attach a motif at the center of the supporting strut at the bottom of the chair in the same way, if desired.

◄ *Two shades of blue – soft duck egg blue and bright Mediterranean sky blue – were used to paint this charming chair. The heart motifs were given a warm 'rusty' glow using metallic waxes in ruby and copper. For your chair, choose paint and wax colors to suit the surrounding decor. If you're overhauling several chairs, it's fun to make each one unique by using an assortment of different colors and motifs.*

CUTWORK PLYWOOD LAMPSHADE

*Create a unique lampshade from plywood panels, cut
in an elegant curved shape with dainty cutwork motifs
and decorated with colorful textured papers.*

This attractive and versatile lampshade design, created from fine plywood and beautiful textured paper, can be adapted to meet all your lighting needs. The instructions show how to make a shade that hangs with lengths of chain from the ceiling; or you can adapt the design slightly to create an elegant shade for a table lamp, as shown above. The design can even be simplified to make smart wall sconces.

The lampshade is constructed from three plywood panels, cut using the templates on page 46. Each panel has a delicate cutwork design backed with handmade paper – when the light is on, it shines through the paper, highlighting the cutwork pattern and the paper's texture. The color of the paper dictates the mood of the lighting – use a rich red or bold orange paper for a warm, welcoming light, or white paper for a cooler feel. You can buy handmade papers at art supply stores; plywood is sold at home improvement centers.

▲ *This smart table lampshade is a variation of the instructions; the finished shade is simply turned upside down and glued on an existing lampshade frame. Before assembling, cut the point from one end of each plywood panel to create the hole in the top of the shade. Use a low-wattage bulb.*

MAKING A LAMPSHADE

The uplighter lampshade is attached to the ceiling using three lengths of chain, which are suspended from three small hooks screwed in place around the light fixture. The length of the chains depends on the height you want the shade to hang in the room; make sure it is at least 6" (15 cm) away from the bulb to prevent scorching. You can buy chain in a range of styles by the yard (meter) at hardware stores.

YOU WILL NEED

- ➤ Tracing paper, thin card and soft pencil
- ➤ Scissors
- ➤ Plywood, 1/16" (1.5 mm)
- ➤ Wood block
- ➤ Drill; 3/8" and 1/8" drill bits
- ➤ Cutting mat, utility knife and metal ruler
- ➤ Sandpaper, fine grade
- ➤ Painter's tape, 3/8" (1 cm) wide
- ➤ Wood stain in antique pine or desired color

- ➤ Soft cloth
- ➤ Textured paper in two colors
- ➤ Double-sided tape
- ➤ 1 to 1 1/2 yd (1 to 1.5 m) of 14 or 18-gauge wire
- ➤ Needlenose pliers
- ➤ Hot glue gun
- ➤ Dimensional paint liner
- ➤ Chain
- ➤ 3 small, screw-in hooks

1 Trace the half-panel template on page 46 onto thin card and cut it out. Lay the card template on the sheet of plywood and draw around it, using a soft pencil. Flip the template and draw around it again to give the whole panel outline; complete with five center holes. Repeat twice to trace three panels on the plywood.

2 Rest the plywood on a wood block, and use a 3/8" drill bit to drill the four large holes in each marked panel. Drill the smaller hole in each panel, using the 3/8" drill bit. Lay the plywood on a cutting mat and carefully cut out each panel, using a utility knife and a metal ruler to guide the blade along the straight edges.

3 Smooth the cut edges of each panel, using fine-grade sandpaper and working right into the corners. Roll the sandpaper into a slim tube and push it into the larger drilled holes to smooth their inner edges.

4 Apply painter's tape along each side of the central cut-out section on one panel, overlapping the tape at the bottom to form a V-shape as shown; make sure the tape edges are pressed down firmly. Apply wood stain to the panel, on each side of the tape, using a soft cloth. Repeat for the remaining two panels.

5 Allow the wood stain to dry, then carefully peel off the painter's tape.

6 Trace the two remaining templates onto thin card and cut them out. Lay the templates onto two different colored papers, draw around each one three times and cut out the shapes.

► Used as a ceiling-hung uplighter, a cutwork plywood lampshade backed with deep red paper creates a handsome focal point and casts a warm, welcoming light over the room. For safety, make sure the bulb hangs at least 6″ (15 cm) away from the shade.

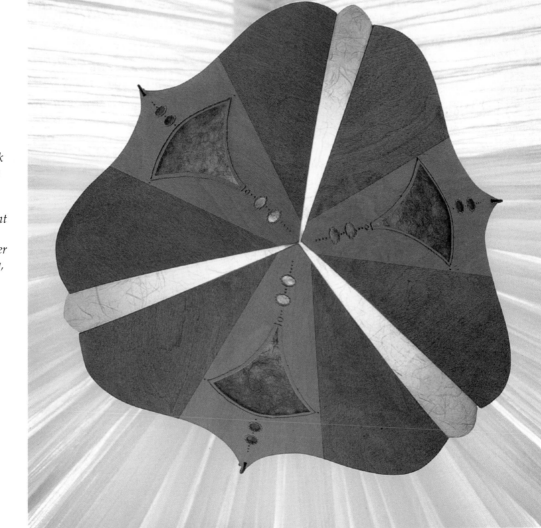

7 Cut several short lengths of double-sided tape and apply them to the back of each plywood panel, around the cutout sections – including the large drilled holes. Apply more double-sided tape around the edges of the larger paper panels. Peel the backing from the tape, and press the paper panels firmly in place over the cutout sections in each plywood panel.

8 Apply a length of double-sided tape to the sides of each plywood panel, on the back. Remove the backing from the tape, and join the three plywood panels, using the remaining paper shapes: press the side edges of the paper onto the tape, using the V at the wide end of the paper as a positioning guide.

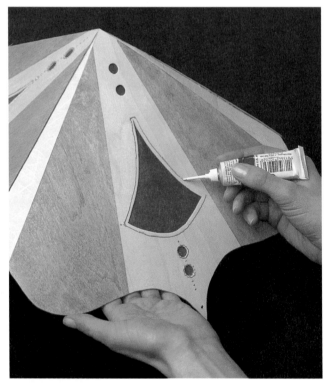

9 Cut 8" (20.5 cm) length of wire. Curl the ends of each wire into a spiral, using needlenose pliers, and shape the center into an arc. Hold one wire against the inside of the lampshade, across the lower edge of one of the joining paper strips. Check the size, then glue in place using a hot glue gun – the wire will strengthen the panel joint. Repeat for two remaining panel joints.

10 Outline the cutout shapes on each panel of the lampshade, using a dimensional liner, and apply additional decorative detailing as desired.

HANGING THE LAMPSHADE

Cut three lengths of chain to the desired length for hanging the shade, using a pair of needlenose pliers to open the links. Cut three short lengths of wire, and bend each one into an S-shape. Hook one end of each S-shape through the small hole in the point of each plywood panel, and slip the other end into the last link of each chain; close the loops in the S-shapes. To hang the shade, screw three small hooks into the ceiling around the light fixture, and slip the free end of each chain onto a hook.

Making a wall light

Cut out, stain and decorate one plywood panel as for **Making a lampshade**, but omit the small drilled hole for hanging. Cut a triangular back plate to the same size as the plywood panel, using 1/2" (1.3 cm) medium-density fiberboard. Drill a hole in each corner of the back plate, using 1/4" drill bit. Cut three 4" (10 cm) lengths of 1/4" (6 mm) dowel, and use wood glue to secure one into each hole drilled in the back plate.

Attach a light fixture onto the back plate, then glue and pin the plywood panel onto the dowel struts. Cover the gap between the back plate and the plywood panel with two lengths of handmade paper, glued around the doweling supports. Mount the light on the wall and insert a low-wattage bulb.

➤ *You can easily adapt the lampshade instructions to create cutwork plywood sconces (see* **Making a wall light**, *above). For a slightly different look, try experimenting with cutwork designs of your own – perhaps repeating a motif or theme already existing in the room.*

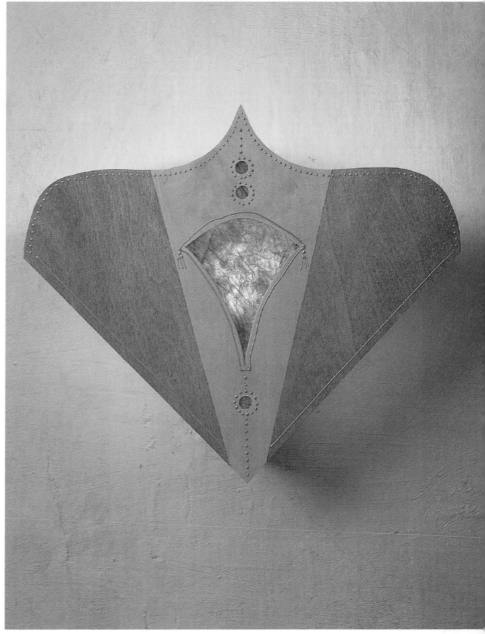

LAMPSHADE TEMPLATES

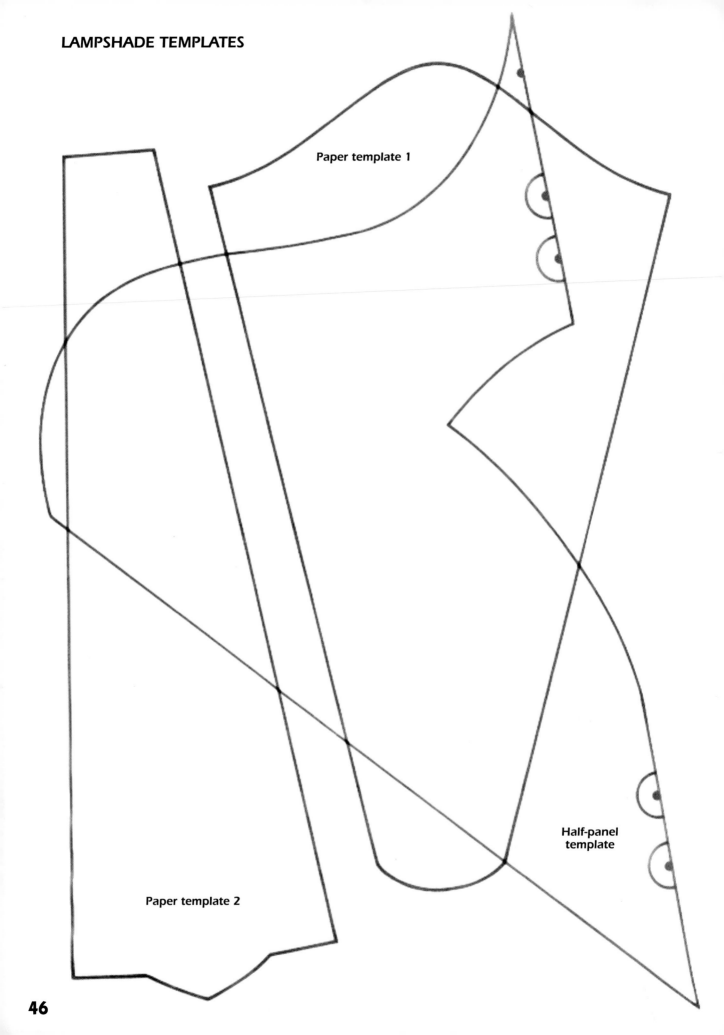

Paper template 1

Paper template 2

Half-panel template

Fabric Works

Fabrics function as a wonderful contrast to the hard, angular surfaces of walls and wood furnishings. Since a wide variety of fabrics are available, they are usually a decorator's primary source of rounded shapes, soft textures, exuberant colors and wild patterns. They provide warmth and privacy and they are necessary to absorb sounds and reduce harsh echoes of everyday living.

Assemble a small fabric wardrobe or stitch a collection of marvelous pillows that reflect your personal style. Create a special set of bed linens, and embellish them with trapunto or Italian quilting. Learn to make a traditional log cabin quilt, and display it on a bed or wall. Protect chair backs with easy yet impressive piecing. Enhance your windows with unique valances, beautiful curtains or beaded blinds. Discover the fun of making the perfect fabric by using a resist technique to paint silks.

FABRIC WARDROBE

*Create an innovative fabric wardrobe using a
traditional wooden clothes drier as the frame, and fitting it
with MDF shelves and a pretty, sheer fabric cover.*

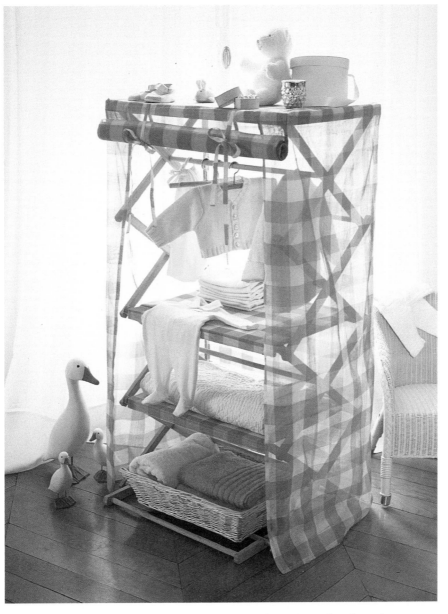

If you're short on storage space for clothes in the bedroom or nursery, but don't have room for a wardrobe or dresser, improvise by using a wooden clothes drier, with shelves and a sheer fabric curtain. The fabric wardrobe is a convenient size, and appears to take up less space than a solid piece of furniture as the translucent cover lets the light filter through.

The clothes drier is glued at each joint to provide a solid framework, and three fabric-covered shelves provide flat storage. These are made from medium-density fiberboard (MDF), with slats that prevent them from sliding off. Two of the clothes drier rails are

sawn out to make room for hanging garments. Only a short hanging space is created – ideal for a baby's or toddler's clothes. If you want a bit more space, you can leave out the middle shelf; alternatively, you can eliminate the hanging space altogether, and simply insert an extra shelf.

The floor-length fabric cover protects the clothes from dust, but allows easy access as the front fabric panel rolls up and is secured with two slim ties. A wide variety of sheer fabrics – including checks, stripes, spots and florals – are available at fabric stores, or you may special-order fabric at an interior design showroom.

▲ *This improvised
fabric wardrobe,
enclosed in a filmy
curtain of checked voile,
is a delightful storage
solution for the nursery.
The hanging space is just
the right size for baby
and toddler garments –
you can even use the
sawn-out rails to make
miniature clothes
hangers (see page 51 for
details). A shallow
wicker basket makes a
useful bottom drawer.*

49

MAKING THE FABRIC WARDROBE

YOU WILL NEED

- Traditional wooden clothes drier
- MDF, 3⁄8" (1 cm)
- Wood slats 3⁄8" x 3⁄4" (1 x 2 cm)
- Sheer fabric
- Hacksaw
- Wood glue
- Sandpaper

- White paint
- Fabric glue
- Paint for clothes hangers (optional)
- Drill and drill bit
- Four large cup hooks
- Matching sewing thread
- Pins

Measuring and cutting out

MDF and slats

Top shelf Set up the clothes drier. Measure the width **(A)** and depth **(B)** of the drier across the uppermost points. Cut a piece of MDF to this size plus 1⁵⁄8" (4 cm) all around, to accommodate the slats and give an overhang for the curtain. Cut two slats to the width of the MDF piece (from side to side), and two to the depth of the MDF piece (from front to back) minus 3⁄4" (2 cm).

Lower shelves Measure the inside width **(C)** and depth **(D)** of the drier at the positions for the two remaining shelves, and add 3⁄4" (2 cm) to the depth measurement only. Cut two pieces of MDF to this size. Also cut four slats to the width of the MDF.

Fabric

Side and back curtain Rest the top shelf on the drier. Measure from the top shelf to the floor, and add 1⁵⁄8" (4 cm) for seams and hems. Measure around the top shelf, from one front corner around the side and back to the other front corner. Add 8" (20.5 cm) for the curtain to wrap around to the front of the drier, plus 2" (5 cm) for

hems. Cut a piece of fabric to these measurements, joining widths using French seams, if necessary.

Front curtain Cut a piece of fabric the width of the top shelf plus 2" (5 cm) for hems, by the height from the top shelf to the floor plus 1⁵⁄8" (4 cm) for seams and hems.

Top shelf cover Cut a piece of fabric the width of the top shelf by the depth, plus 5⁄8" (1.5 cm) all around for seams.

Lower shelf covers Cut two pieces of fabric the width of the lower shelves by their depth plus 2¾" (7 cm) all around.

Fabric ties Cut two strips of fabric 1⁵⁄8" x 40" (4 x 102 cm).

PREPARING THE CLOTHES DRIER

1 Use a hacksaw and hold the clothes drier firmly to cut out the central rail, second from the top; saw close to each end. Repeat to remove the front rail, second from the top. Set rails aside. This makes room for hanging garments, suspended from the top central rail.

2 Apply wood glue to the cut rail ends, and allow to dry. This prevents the ends of the rails from slipping out and the drier from collapsing. Apply glue to all the remaining joints to make the drier into a solid, non-folding framework.

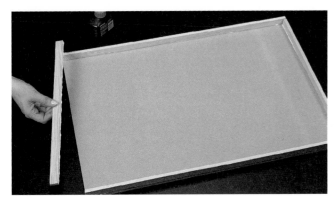

3 Lay the two long slats along the front and back edges of the top shelf, and the two short ones along the short edges; place each slat's narrower edge against the shelf, and align the outer edges of the slats and shelf. Glue in place; allow to dry.

4 Glue the four remaining slats along the front and back edges of the two lower shelves, as in step 3. Allow to dry.

5 Paint the shelves and slats white, and allow to dry. Lay one of the fabric pieces for the lower shelves out flat, wrong side up. Center a shelf facedown on the fabric. Wrap the fabric over the slats, and glue it in place, using fabric glue; glue the corners around the ends of the slats, trimming the fabric where necessary and folding it under to lie flat. Glue the short fabric edges to the underside of the shelf. Repeat for the second lower shelf. (The top shelf is covered at a later stage.) Allow to dry.

6 Position the top shelf on the clothes drier and secure it with wood glue. Position the lower shelves across the first and second set of parallel rails, and secure with wood glue. Allow to dry.

MAKING CLOTHES HANGERS

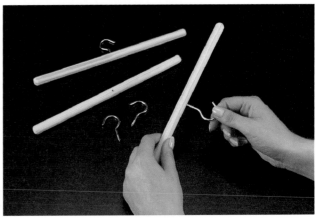

1 Measure and mark halfway along the two rails that were removed from the clothes drier; saw through the rails at this point. Sand the cut ends smooth, giving them a slightly rounded finish. If desired, paint the four lengths of rail.

2 Mark and drill a pilot hole halfway along each of the lengths of rail. Screw a large hook into each hole to make a clothes hanger.

MAKING THE FABRIC COVER

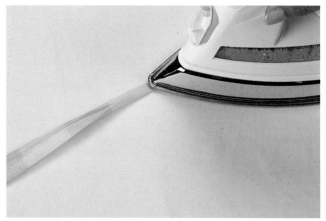

1 Press under a double ½" (1.3 cm) hem on both sides and along the lower edge of the side and back curtain. Machine-stitch in place. Repeat to hem the side and lower edges of the front curtain.

2 Press ⅜" (1 cm) to the wrong side along both long edges of each fabric tie. Tuck in the short ends; fold the ties in half lengthwise to enclose all the raw edges. Press. Machine-stitch the long edges and across both short ends of the ties to secure.

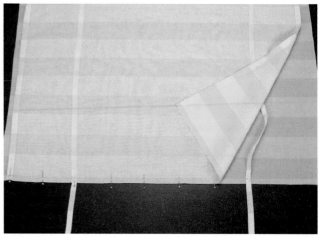

3 Lay the top shelf cover out flat, right side up. Measure and pin-mark 6½" (16.3 cm) in from each corner along the front edge. Pin and tack a fabric tie at each marked point, securing the tie halfway along its length.

4 Center the top unhemmed edge of the front curtain on the front edge of the top shelf cover, right sides together and raw edges even.

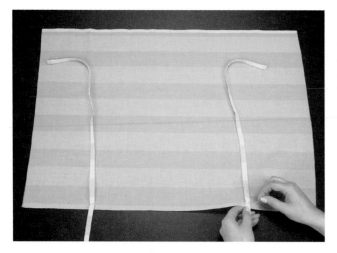

5 Measure and mark with a pin halfway along the back edge of the top shelf cover. Also measure and mark halfway along the top, unhemmed edge of the side and back curtain. Lay the side and back curtain over the top shelf cover, right sides together and raw edges even, matching the pin marks. Pin all around, clipping into the curtain to ease the corners; the side and back curtain should extend a short way around to the front edge of the top cover at each corner, enclosing the front curtain. Machine-stitch ⅝" (1.5 cm) seams around the top shelf cover.

6 Turn the wardrobe cover right side out; press. Hang it over the clothes drier. Roll up the front curtain and secure it at the desired height, using the fabric ties.

BOLSTER PILLOWS

Capture the elegance of regal beds and sofas by making a pair
of tailored bolster pillows. These are deceptively easy to make yet
look wonderful and provide instant sophistication.

Bolster pillows were traditionally used as supports at each end of a daybed or chaise longue. You can buy the forms in fabric stores, or make your own by rolling a length of thick polyester fleece to the desired shape and slipstitching it securely in place.

The cover for your bolster pillow can be as simple or as decorative as you like. The instructions show how to make a neat, tailored cover with flat end pieces, and a more lavish cover with gathered ends and a decorative fabric-covered button or tassel. Covered piping emphasizes the structure of the pillow and gives a smart finish. Use the main fabric

for the covered piping, or opt for a plain, coordinating color, or one that links the pillow with existing soft furnishings.

The main body of the cover is cut from just one rectangle of fabric, joined along the length by a long zipper to ensure easy removal for laundering. For a tailored cover, you'll need two circular end pieces which you can cut with the aid of a compass; for a gathered-end cover you'll just need two slim rectangles of fabric, one for each end. For best results the cover should fit the pillow form snugly, to give a firm, tailored shape.

Whether you make a tailored bolster pillow with flat end pieces or a more elaborate-looking one with gathered ends, you'll find your pillow invaluable. Bolsters provide excellent support for your back or neck and make a welcome change from basic square pillows.

TAILORED BOLSTER COVER

YOU WILL NEED

- Bolster pillow form or thick fleece rolled and stitched to make a form
- Decorator fabric
- Compass and pencil
- Tape measure, scissors, dressmaker pins
- Zipper, 2" (5 cm) shorter than form
- Sewing thread to match main fabric
- Zipper foot
- Piping cord
- Fabric to cover the piping cord

Measuring and cutting out

Main piece Measure the length and circumference of your bolster pillow form, taking your second measurement near the circular end of the pad for accuracy. Add 1¼" (3.2 cm) to each measurement; cut rectangle to this size, making sure the pattern will run in the desired direction on the bolster.

End pieces Measure the diameter of the bolster form, or take this measurement from the package label. Divide this measurement by two, and add ⅝" (1.5 cm) for seam allowances. Draw two circles on the wrong side of your fabric, using compass; position circles so the fabric design is centered, or as well balanced as possible. Cut out each circle along the marked line.

Covered piping Cut two strips of fabric on the bias, the diameter of your piping cord plus 1¼" (3.2 cm) for seams, by the circumference of the bolster pad plus 1½" (3.8 cm) to allow for joining the ends.

1 Fold the main piece in half lengthwise, with right sides together; pin at intervals to hold the fabric in position. Center the zipper along the long raw edges. Pin-mark the zipper ends and machine-stitch up to the marks at each end, taking a ⅝" (1.5 cm) seam; backstitch at the ends to strengthen them. Baste along the zipper stitching line, finish the raw edges, and press the seam open.

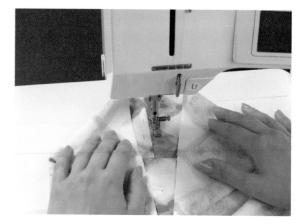

2 Lay the fabric with the seam allowance up; position the zipper facedown on top. Pin and baste in place, taking care not to catch the fabric on the other side of the cover. Stitch down each side of the zipper and across the ends, using zipper foot. Remove the basting and check that the zipper runs smoothly.

3 Staystitch around each free end of the fabric tube, stitching ½" (1.3 cm) from the raw edges. Snip into the seam allowance at regular intervals, about every ¾" (2 cm); cut up to but not through the staystitching, using sharp scissors. This provides the ease you will need to attach the end pieces neatly to the fabric tube.

4 Fold piping strip around cord, wrong sides together, matching raw edges. Machine-baste close to cording, using zipper foot. Pin piping to right side of each end piece, matching raw edges; snip seam allowance as necessary. Lap ends of the piping fabric where they meet and trim the cord so the ends butt together. Stitch the piping in place.

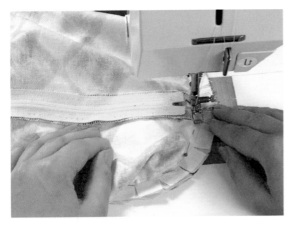

5 Open the zipper slightly. Pin each end piece to the open ends of the main piece, right sides together and raw edges even; position the zipper seam at the bottom of each end piece if the fabric is directional. Stitch around each end piece, working with the main piece on top and stitching very close to the piping, using zipper foot.

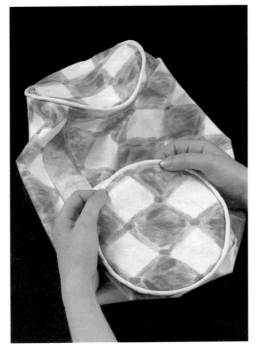

6 Clip the seam allowances of the end pieces to reduce bulk, if necessary. Grade the seams of very thick fabrics by trimming more fabric from the seam allowances of the end pieces. Turn the cover right side out through the zipper opening. Insert the pillow form, and close the zipper.

BOLSTER WITH GATHERED ENDS

YOU WILL NEED

➤ Bolster pillow form, or thick fleece rolled and stitched to make a form

➤ Decorator fabric

➤ Piping cord

➤ Fabric to cover the piping cord

➤ Sewing thread to match main fabric

➤ Matching zipper 2" (5 cm) shorter than the form

➤ Tape measure, scissors, dressmaker pins

➤ Zipper foot

➤ Two buttons-to-cover, or tassels

Measuring and cutting out

Main piece Follow the instructions for the **Tailored bolster cover** to cut one piece from your chosen decorator fabric to fit the bolster form. Cut directional fabric so that the pattern will run in the desired direction on the cover.

End pieces Measure the circumference and diameter of your bolster form. Cut two rectangles the circumference of the bolster plus 1 1/4" (3.2 cm) by half the diameter plus 1 1/4" (3.2 cm). The fabric pattern usually works best if the pattern runs along the length of each rectangle, so bear this in mind when planning and cutting out the two end pieces.

Covered piping Follow the cutting instructions for the **Tailored bolster cover** to cut two strips of fabric on the bias.

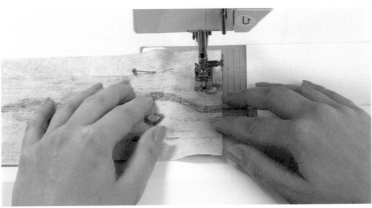

1 Fold the main fabric piece in half, right sides together; stitch the seam and insert the zipper as for the **Tailored bolster cover**, steps 1-2. Fold each end piece in half, right sides together and short ends matched. Stitch across the short ends, taking a 5/8" (1.5 cm) seam allowance. Finish the seam allowances, using zigzag or serger. Press the seam open.

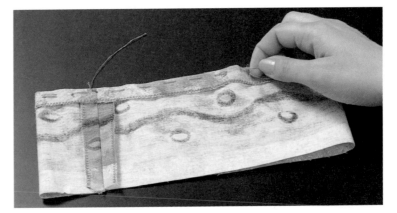

2 Finish one long edge of each end piece. Press under 5/8" (1.5 cm) along these edges. Work two parallel rows of gathering stitches close to the pressed edge, using doubled matching thread; don't stitch too far from the pressed edge, or your stitches may show on the right side. Cover cording as for the **Tailored bolster cover**, step 4.

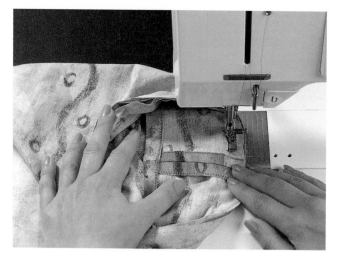

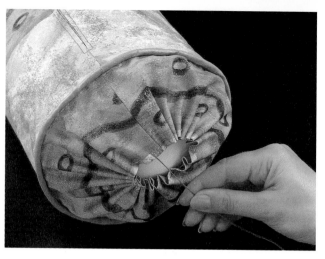

3 Pin one piece of covered piping to each open end of the main piece, raw edges matching and cord ends meeting at the zipper seam. Join the ends as on page 54, step 4. Stitch the piping using the zipper foot. Pin one end piece to each free end of the main piece, right sides together and raw edges matching. Stitch around the end piece, taking a 5/8" (1.5 cm) seam allowance; stitch close to the piping, using zipper foot.

4 Trim the seam allowances to different widths to reduce bulk of thick fabrics. Turn the cover right side out and insert the form. Gently but firmly pull up the gathering threads at each end; thread the ends onto a needle and take a few stitches, pulling the thread tight to hold the gathers in place. Knot the thread securely, take the ends to the wrong side of the cover, and trim close.

5 Choose two buttons-to-cover that are large enough to hide the center ring of gathering stitches. Cover the two buttons with matching or contrasting fabric, following the manufacturer's instructions. Stitch one button securely to the center of each gathered end of the cover. Or, substitute a pair of matching decorative tassels for the buttons.

Crisp checks suit the smartly tailored finish of bolster pillows, and complement both formal and relaxed room schemes. Note how, on the gathered end of this colorful bolster, the checks fan out to create an attractive design of concentric circles.

No chaise longue is complete without a bolster pillow to highlight its graceful curves and give comfy support. This gathered-end bolster echoes the broad-striped upholstery of the chaise, but uses a fresher blue and green colorway.

BUTTONED PILLOWS

Add an up-to-the-minute touch to pillow covers with clever seaming and decorative buttons and loops. Choose fresh floral print fabrics or smart brocades.

One of the quickest and most effective ways of brightening up a room is to make new pillow covers or liven up existing old ones. Pillow covers can supply the missing link in a decorative scheme, introducing fresh colors and patterns or tying together the different shades of your existing furnishings. Bold fabrics that you may avoid using on a large scale can look stunning in small

quantities. And, since you need less than a yard of fabric to make a pillow cover, you can easily tailor your fabric to suit your budget – splurging for a fairly extravagant fabric or making use of remnants.

Although these covers look quite ornate they are very simple to make. The buttons and loops on the front of the covers are purely decorative so there are no fiddly buttonholes to

work; and the overlapped opening at the back conceals the pillow form and means there's no need for a zipper or other fastener.

▼ *Pillow covers in bright spring colors bring a breath of fresh air to this living room. Buttons in a variety of shapes and colors, and complementary loops, add a lively finishing touch.*

MAKING A BUTTONED-FRONT PILLOW

Measuring and cutting out

For a standard pillow cover 18" (46 cm) square, you will need ⅝ yd (0.6 m) of fabric.

Measure one side of the pillow form.

Front panels Cut one rectangle of fabric the width of the form plus 1" (2.5 cm) seam allowance by the width of the form less 4" (10 cm). Cut another rectangle 7" (18 cm) by the width of the form plus 1" (2.5 cm) for seam allowance.
Cut the two front panels from two different fabrics, if desired.

Back panels Cut two rectangles the width of the form plus 1" (2.5 cm) seam allowance by half the width plus 3¼" (8.2 cm) back opening allowance.

YOU WILL NEED

➤ Fabric

➤ Matching sewing thread

➤ Five buttons

➤ Pillow form

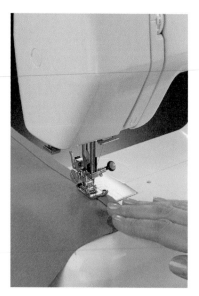

1 Press under 1" (2.5 cm) along one long edge of the larger front panel. Place the smaller front panel right side up. Position the pressed edge of the larger panel over one long edge of the smaller front panel with raw edges matching. Pin and baste the panels together along the folded edge.

2 Stitch the front panels together, topstitching ¼" (6 mm) and ¾" (2 cm) from the pressed folded edge.

3 Turn under a double ⅜" (1 cm) hem along one long edge of each back panel. Pin and stitch in place.

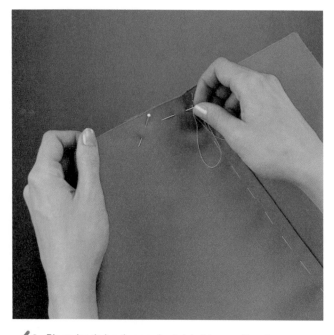

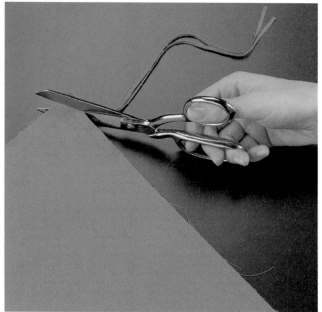

4 Place both back panels right side up. Overlap one hemmed edge with the other by 3¼" (8.2 cm); align raw ends. Baste the overlapped edges together.

5 Place the front and back pieces together, right sides together and raw edges matching. Pin and stitch all around the outside edges, taking a ½" (1.3 cm) seam allowance. Trim the seams to ⅜" (1 cm); clip diagonally across the corners.

6 Remove the basting and turn the cover right side out. Press flat with the seam pulled out to the edge. Edgestitch all around the cover, using the presser foot as a guide.

7 On the front of the cover, mark the center of the topstitched seam, between the two rows of stitching. Mark two more points to each side of the center so that there are five points all the same distance apart. Hand-sew a button at each point. Insert the pillow form through the back opening.

MAKING A BUTTON-LOOP PILLOW

1 Cut out and prepare the front and back fabric pieces following **Making a buttoned-front pillow,** steps 1-4; omit the second row of topstitching on the front unit.

YOU WILL NEED

➤ Fabric

➤ Matching sewing thread

➤ Three buttons

➤ 1 ⅛ yd (1.05 m) decorative cord

➤ Pillow form

2 Measure and mark the center of a back edge that is parallel to the hemmed edges. Mark a point to each side of this point, halfway between the center and the adjoining side. Cut the cord into three equal lengths. Fold each length in half to make a loop. Position one loop at each marked point so the cut ends are aligned with the raw edge of the fabric. Pin and tack in place.

3 Stitch the front and back panels together, following **Making a buttoned-front pillow,** steps 5 and 6; match back edge with loops to narrow side of front unit. Bring the loops to the front of the cover and mark the positions for the buttons. Sew a button at each mark and hook the loops over the buttons. Insert a pillow form through the back opening.

▲ Complement a traditional room with rich jewel-colored brocade pillows. Add gilt buttons and metallic cords to complete the classic look.

◀ Fabrics shot through with gold thread look superb with ornamental buttons and multicolored cord. Use small fabric motifs and metal-edged buttons-to-cover for a tailored, professional finish.

BLANKET PILLOWS

Woolly blankets make super-soft covers for casual pillows. Combine two contrasting colored blankets to create a bold, contemporary look. Or use the blanket's fringed edge for a relaxed look.

If you like the warm, snug feel of blankets and throws on your sofas and chairs, why not make some pillow covers to match? The designs shown here use blankets in two contrasting solid colors: one for the pillow front, and one for the pillow back and the appliqué square on the front. If you don't have any suitable blankets on hand, you can buy a coating fabric to match your color scheme. Wool is the most durable choice, but acrylic and other synthetic fibers make a good, inexpensive and easy care alternative.

The size and color of the appliqué square give the pillow its character. You can make the appliqué square as large or as small as you wish. A tiny lime-green square on a tangerine pillow makes an amusing focal point, for example, while a large cream-colored square on a beige background gives a pillow a classic feel. In the 18" (46 cm) pillow shown below, the finished size of the terra-cotta appliqué is 5⅛" (12.8 cm) square, and the green appliqué is 12" (30.5 cm) square.

The back and front pillow pieces are joined together using the blanket stitch, which adds decorative detail and creates a neat, flat outline around the outside edge. To show off the stitching to advantage, the finished covers are slightly larger than the pillow forms. Work the blanket stitch in the colors of the blankets, or introduce another shade for greater emphasis. To create a fringed envelope pillow, see page 64.

▼ *This pair of pillows looks cozy and inviting at the head of a bed. The blanket fabric introduces a soft texture to the contemporary interior.*

MAKING A BLANKET-STITCHED PILLOW

For one 18¾" (48 cm) square pillow cover:

- ➤ Two contrasting colored blankets, or two coating fabrics, 60" (150 cm) wide: ⅝ yd (0.6 m) of fabric A and ½ yd (0.5 m) of fabric B
- ➤ Tape measure
- ➤ Scissors, pins
- ➤ Matching sewing thread (optional)
- ➤ Hand sewing needle and basting thread
- ➤ Crewel needle
- ➤ Contrasting decorative thread or multi-ply embroidery wool yarn
- ➤ Dressmaker's pencil or pen
- ➤ Toggle or large button
- ➤ 18" (46 cm) square pillow form

Measuring and cutting out

Cut all the fabric pieces on the straight grain. Use one of the blankets or fabrics for the pillow front (fabric A) and the other for the appliqué square and the pillow back (fabric B).

From fabric A Cut one 20" (51 cm) square for the pillow front.

From fabric B Cut one appliqué square to the desired size plus ⅝" (1.5 cm) all around for seam allowances. For the pillow back, cut one 13¼" x 20" (33.5 x 51 cm) rectangle and one 10¼" x 20" (26.1 x 51 cm) rectangle, placing one long edge on the selvage, if possible. Finish one long edge of the larger back piece with machine zigzag stitch, if not cut on selvage.

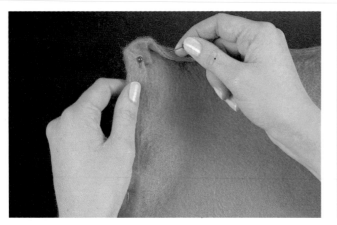

1 Pin under ⅝" (1.5 cm) all around the pillow front; fold in the corner before turning under the sides to miter each corner. Press square to set the hems; baste hems. Repeat for the appliqué square, if desired.

2 With right sides up, center the appliqué square on top of the pillow front. Pin and baste the appliqué square in place.

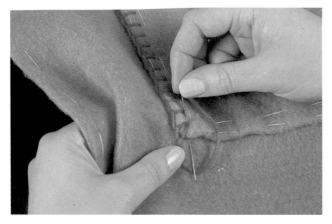

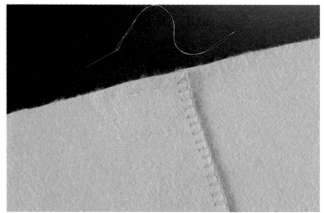

3 Use a crewel needle and decorative thread or two strands of embroidery wool to work blanket stitch all around the edge of the appliqué square, starting at the center of one side. At each corner, work one stitch diagonally to the same point as the stitches on either side. Remove basting from the appliqué square.

4 Pin under ⅝" (1.5 cm) along one long edge of the smaller back piece; baste. Work blanket stitch along this hemmed edge. Remove basting. With right sides up, lap the blanket-stitched edge over the selvage or finished edge of the larger back piece, until the total width is 20" (51 cm). Pin the back pieces together at each end of the overlap; baste inside the seam allowances.

A blanket-stitched overlap makes the pillow back as eye-catching as the front. Finish with a large, decorative button or toggle for the closure.

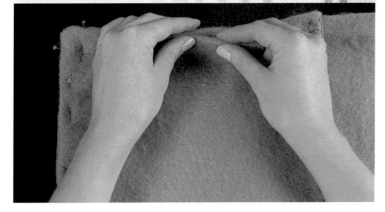

5 Center the pillow back on top of the pillow front, wrong sides together. Turn in and pin the edges of the pillow back so that they line up with the pillow front, mitering the corners as in step 1 (opposite). Baste securely all around the edge, through all four layers.

6 Starting at the center of one side, work blanket stitch all around the outside edge, pushing the needle vertically through the layers to ensure that the stitches are the same size on both sides of the pillow. Work the corners as in step 3 (opposite). Remove basting.

Making a thread loop

Thread loops are a decorative option for securing buttons and toggles, and can be used when the fabric edges overlap. They are made by stitching a foundation loop of thread at the edge of the fabric, then working blanket stitch along the loop. If you are using regular thread to make the thread loop, double it.

1 Add together the diameter and depth of the button, or the length and depth of the toggle, to calculate the length of the loop. Mark the position for ends of the loop on the fabric, using dressmaker's pencil or pen.

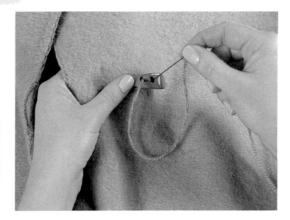

2 Secure the thread at one mark with a few small backstitches on the wrong side. Bring the needle to the right side at this mark, and take a stitch at the second mark to form a foundation loop the length calculated in step 1 above. Make 1-3 more loops, according to the thickness of your thread. Secure with a backstitch on the wrong side.

7 Using one strand of yarn, work a thread loop at the center of the blanket-stitched edge of the back overlap, as shown in **Making a thread loop** (left). Stitch the toggle or button to the back underlap, to correspond with the loop. Insert the pillow form.

3 Shape the working thread into a loop, insert the needle underneath the foundation loops and pull it through over the working thread to form a blanket stitch. Continue to work blanket stitches along the length of the foundation loop. Secure the thread with two small backstitches through the fabric; trim the thread ends close.

▼ *A small contrasting appliqué square adds a witty touch to this blanket pillow.*

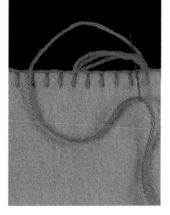

MAKING A FRINGED ENVELOPE PILLOW

If you have a woolen blanket that is trimmed with decorative fringe, make a feature of it by stitching the envelope pillow shown here. You simply cut a rectangle of fabric with the fringe at one short end, fold the short ends to overlap in the center, and stitch around the outside edge.

YOU WILL NEED

For one 18" (46 cm) square pillow cover:

➤ Blanket with a fringed edge

➤ Tape measure

➤ Scissors

➤ Pins

➤ Matching sewing thread

➤ 18" (46 cm) square pillow form

Measuring and cutting out

If your blanket has an obvious pattern, such as a check or plaid, wrap the blanket around the pillow form first, to determine where the design will fall when the fringe is positioned along the center of the pillow. Cut separate pieces for the pillow, as described in **Positioning the pattern** (below), if necessary. **From the blanket**, cut one 19¼" x 40" (49.1 x 102 cm) rectangle, positioning the fringe at one short end.

1 Finish plain short end of fabric, using zigzag or serger. Lay the fabric flat, right side up. Fold the short ends to meet in the center, then lap the plain end over the fringed end by 4" (10 cm). Cut off the fringe that falls within the seam allowances.

2 Pin raw edges together; make sure fringe does not fall into seam allowances. Machine-stitch, taking a ⅝" (1.5 cm) seam allowance. Trim the corners. Turn the pillow cover right side out and insert the pillow form.

TIP

Positioning the pattern

To position the fabric design precisely on the pillow cover, you may need to cut separate pieces. Center your chosen parts of the design on the following pieces: for the pillow back, cut one 19" (48.5 cm) square; for the pillow front, cut one 9½" x 19" (24.3 x 48.5 cm) rectangle, with the fringe at one short end, and one 13½" x 19 (34.3 x 48.5 cm) rectangle. Pin the front pieces to the back, right sides together, with the plain end lapped over the fringed end, and stitch all around as in step 2 above.

▲ *A fringed envelope pillow made from a colorful checked blanket is a cheerful accessory for the home. For a coordinated look, drape a matching blanket throw behind the pillow.*

PILLOWCASES

Coordinated bed linen creates an attractive focal point in your bedroom. Making your own pillowcases allows you to choose from a wide variety of fabrics to give an exciting mix-and-match look.

Making your own pillowcases is easy, even for beginners, and allows you to create a coordinated style for your bed linen.

A duvet cover, bedspread or throw is likely to be your starting point. You can pick out one of the colors from it and use a solid fabric in this shade for the pillowcases. Or emphasize the differences with pillowcases in a contrasting color or a fresh, new pattern – checks and stripes to balance an exuberant floral, for example.

Directions for two styles of pillowcase are included: a standard, straight-edged case with an inner flap to hold the pillow in place; and a pillowcase with a double-sided ruffle around the outside for a softer, more feminine look. You can use matching or contrasting fabric for the ruffle; make sure the ruffle fabric has the same care requirements as the pillowcase fabric.

▲ *A colorful blend of mix-and-match fabrics, including floral checks and stripes, dresses this bed in style. You can choose fabrics from a manufacturer's coordinated collection to make your pillowcases, or put together your own exciting combinations.*

MAKING PILLOWCASES

Choosing fabric

Bed linen has to be practical as well as pretty, so make sure your chosen fabric is machine washable. Pure cotton is a popular choice for bed linen, but needs thorough pressing to look its best. Polyester-cotton blends are an easy-care option – look for polyester-cotton sheeting, which is generally inexpensive and comes in a wide range of solid colors and coordinating prints.

Wash the fabric to pre-shrink it before you begin cutting out the pillowcases.

YOU WILL NEED

➤ Sheeting fabric or other, easy-care cotton or cotton blend fabric

➤ Tape measure

➤ Scissors

➤ Pins

➤ Matching sewing thread

For a ruffled pillowcase:

➤ Fabric for ruffle

MAKING A BASIC PILLOWCASE

Measuring and cutting out

Measure the sides of the pillow. A standard pillow is 20" x 30" (51 x 76 cm).

Cutting fabric Cut a rectangle of fabric the width of the pillow plus 1 1/2" (3.8 cm) by twice the length of the pillow plus 8 1/4" (21.2 cm).

1 Press under 1/4" (6 mm) and then 1 1/4" (3.2 cm) on one short edge of the fabric rectangle. Pin and machine-stitch close to the inner fold. Press under and pin a double 3/8" (1 cm) hem on the other short edge. Machine-stitch close to the inner fold.

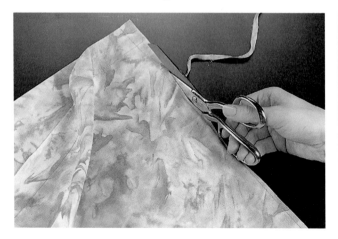

2 Fold and press narrow hemmed edge 6" (15 cm) to the wrong side. Fold the fabric so the other hemmed edge meets the pressed edge, wrong sides together and raw edges aligned. Pin and machine-stitch the raw edges, taking a 1/2" (1.3 cm) seam. Trim the seams to 1/4" (6 mm).

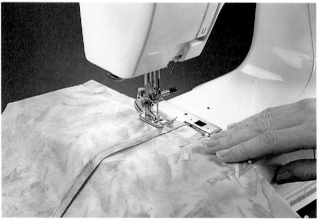

3 Turn the pillowcase wrong side out, including the flap. Machine-stitch, 1/2" (1.3 cm) from each long edge, to enclose the raw edges, forming a French seam. Turn the pillowcase right side out and press.

MAKING A RUFFLED PILLOWCASE

Measuring and cutting out

Measure the pillow.

Front panel Cut a rectangle of fabric the length of the pillow plus 1" (2.5 cm) by the width plus 1" (2.5 cm).

Back panel Cut a rectangle of fabric the length of the pillow plus 1¼" (3.2 cm) by the width plus 1" (2.5 cm).

Overlap panel Cut a rectangle of fabric 8" (20.5 cm) deep by the width of the pillow plus 1" (2.5 cm).

Ruffle Cut 7" (18 cm) wide fabric strips to make a continuous loop of the required length: one-and-a-half times the circumference of the pillow.

TIP

Lacy finish

Instead of a ruffle, you can add a lace or eyelet trim around the edge of the pillowcase. Trims are sold in a variety of styles in fabric stores. Stitch the lace trim in place in the same way as the ruffle, either gathering it or leaving it flat to show off the pattern; if you decide to stitch the trim on flat, allow a little extra ease to pleat around the corners.

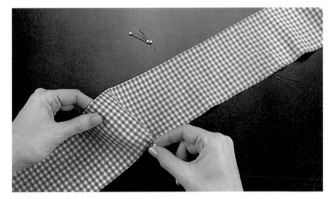

1 Seam the fabric strips for the ruffle to make a loop. Press the seams open. Fold the strip in half lengthwise, wrong sides together, and press. Divide the loop into four equal sections, and mark the sections with pins at the raw edges.

2 Sew two rows of gathering stitches along the raw edges of the ruffle loop, through both layers of fabric, starting and stopping at each pin; position one row of stitching ¼" (6 mm) from the raw edges, and the other ½" (1.3 cm) from the raw edges.

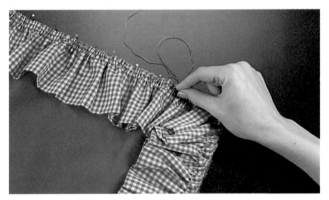

3 Lay the front pillowcase panel right side up, and mark the midpoint of each side edge with a pin. Pin the ruffle to the right side of the front panel, matching the pins and the raw edges. Pull up the threads to gather the ruffle so that it fits the front panel; ease extra fullness into the corners. Pin ruffle in place; baste.

4 Press under and stitch a double ⅜" (1 cm) hem on one short edge of the back panel. Press under and stitch a double ⅜" (1 cm) hem on one long edge of the overlap panel. Place the back panel on the front panel, with right sides together and raw edges matching. Position the overlap panel, right side down, over the hemmed edge of the back panel, so that the raw edges of the overlap and front panels are matching. Pin all around the outer edges of the pillowcase.

5 Stitch around the outside edges of the pillowcase, taking a ½" (1.3 cm) seam allowance. Trim the seam allowances and clip across the corners. Finish the seams, using zigzag or serger. Turn right side out and press.

The clean lines of checked fabrics suit the simple style of the inner flap pillowcase. Here, a mix of large and small-scale checks adds an interesting twist.

Simple, straight-edged pillowcases in solid fabrics repeat the colors of the checked pillowcases. White buttons add a smart detail along the opening edge of the black pillowcases; if you don't have time to sew buttonholes, you can simply stitch the buttons to the front of the pillowcase as a false closure.

A soft ruffle is perfect for pillowcases in pretty floral fabrics. You can make the ruffle from the same fabric as the pillowcase, use a solid fabric in one of the colors from the print, or choose a dainty eyelet or lace trim for a romantic touch.

FLANGED PILLOWCASES

A flanged pillowcase is a bedroom classic that will never go out of style. Make a set from fresh crisp cotton using the clever minimum sewing method featured below.

Flanged pillowcases have an appealing simplicity that suits most room styles. The flange is created by folding and mitering the front section of fabric over the back.

The key to creating a successful pillowcase is cutting and pressing accurately. Make sure you cut all the sections on the grain, otherwise the finished pillowcase may pull out of shape with use. It's also important to press the hems carefully before stitching, as this makes the sewing easier and you'll get much neater results.

You can make your pillowcase from any machine-washable decorator or sheeting fabric. Cotton or polyester-cotton fabrics are ideal because they press well and give a crisp finish.

The instructions are for a pillowcase to fit a queen pillow 30" x 20" (76 x 51 cm). The central pocket of the pillowcase is slightly smaller – 29½" x 18½" (74.8 x 47.3 cm) to create a plump look when the pillow is inserted.

A white flanged pillowcase is a bedroom classic that will never go out of style, but for fashionable chic why not add a decorative flange? This one is cut from striped shirting fabric. Make a plain flanged pillowcase first, and then you will see how easy it is to create variations.

Flanges add instant sophistication to pillowcases and lend a real professional finish. Their stylish simplicity suits plain, cotton fabrics; make them in traditional white, as above, or single colors to match your bedding. For extra detailing, add decorative machine stitching, as below.

MAKING A FLANGED PILLOWCASE

- ➤ Decorator or sheeting fabric
- ➤ Matching sewing thread
- ➤ Tape measure, scissors, pins

Measuring and cutting out

Front Cut a 38" x 27¼" (96.5 x 69 cm) rectangle of fabric. This allows for a 2" (5 cm) deep flange. For a 3" (7.5 cm) flange, add an extra 4" (10 cm) to each dimension.

Back Cut a 31" x 19¾" (78.5 x 50.5 cm) rectangle.

Flap Cut a 7" x 19¾" (18 x 50.5 cm) rectangle.

1 Turn under and press 3⁄8" (1 cm) and then 5⁄8" (1.5 cm) on one long edge of the flap. Pin the pressed hem in place; stitch close to the inner fold. Repeat on one short edge of the back piece.

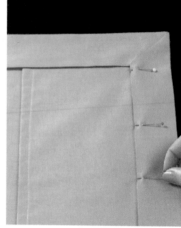

2 Turn under and press 3⁄8" (1 cm), and then 2" (5 cm) on each edge of the front piece. If you cut fabric for a 3" (7.5 cm) flange, press under 3⁄8" (1 cm) and then 3" (7.5 cm). Unfold the fabric. Fold each corner diagonally, as shown. Press the fold, and trim the corners 5⁄8" (1.5 cm) outside this fold.

3 Fold each corner of the front piece diagonally, right sides together. Stitch the corner miters, starting at the folded edge and stopping at the outer pressed lines.

4 Trim the corner miter seams and turn right side out. Turn in the raw edges of the flange along the outer pressed lines. Slip the hemmed flap 5⁄8" (1.5 cm) under one end of the flange to conceal the raw edges. Pin the long edge of the flap in place; baste.

5 Slip the back piece under the flange; all raw edges should extend under the flange 5⁄8" (1.5 cm). The hemmed end of the back piece should be about 1⁄8" (3 mm) away from the flange at the flap end of the pillowcase. Pin the back piece in place.

6 Machine-stitch the flange in place along the inner edge, using a straight stitch or a decorative machine stitch; if you use a decorative stitch, make sure it's a stitch that looks good on both sides. Remove the basting and press the finished pillowcase.

ITALIAN AND TRAPUNTO QUILTING

*Create subtle three-dimensional designs on pillowcases, pillow
covers and other soft furnishings, using the traditional
techniques of Italian and trapunto quilting.*

Most quilting techniques were developed as a means of keeping layers of fabric and batting together for warmth or protection, but Italian and trapunto quilting have always been purely decorative. Italian quilting, also called corded quilting, is the easiest of the two methods. It is created by stitching a loosely woven fabric to the back of the main fabric in a design made up of narrow channels. These are then filled with yarn or cord. Filling the channels with yarn creates a more subtle effect and is very soft, making it ideal for bedding items and pillows. Cord is a firmer filling and

therefore creates stronger design lines, but it's also harder to the touch.

Trapunto quilting is created in a similar way, but the design can be any size or shape. Instead of using cord, you stuff the shapes with fiberfill, inserting it through holes or slits made in the backing fabric. Polyester fiberfill is the best filling because it is light and washable. Use muslin for the backing fabric – its loosely woven threads make it easy to push the stuffing in, and it is inexpensive.

The steps on the following pages show how to create a pretty daisy design for a flanged pillowcase, using Italian quilting for the stems and

▲ *Italian quilting techniques can be as complex or simple as you like. The single daisy flower on the blue pillowcase was hand-stitched in a contrasting embroidery cotton to give it greater impact, while the more elaborate design on the white pillowcase was created on a sewing machine.*

trapunto quilting for the leaves and flowers. You can adapt the design as you like, stitching the whole design or just a single daisy flower. The design is completed before the flanged pillowcase is assembled.

FLANGED PILLOWCASE WITH QUILTED MOTIFS

Before you start

Wash the muslin, main fabric and lining; otherwise the fabrics may shrink at different rates when you wash them later, making the finished piece pucker and pull out of shape. Decide whether you are going to stitch the design by hand or machine. Working on a machine is quicker, but on intricate designs you may find it easier to work by hand. Details for both techniques are given in the steps. Practice on scrap fabrics first.

Cutting out

Queen-size pillowcase Cut the flanged pillowcase front, back and flap as on page 70.

Muslin backing Cut one 31" x 19¾" (78.5 x 50.5 cm) rectangle. (If the design will be on something other than a flanged pillowcase, cut the muslin the same size as the main fabric.)

Lining Cut one rectangle the same size as the muslin backing.

YOU WILL NEED

➤ Decorator or sheeting fabric

➤ Muslin

➤ Pins, sewing thread

➤ Transfer pencil, tape measure

➤ Quilting thread, or embroidery cotton and embroidery hoop (optional)

➤ Small, sharp scissors

➤ Pointed tweezers, toothpick or stylus

➤ Polyester fiberfill

➤ Hand sewing needle, large tapestry needle

➤ Yarn or soft cord

QUILTING THE DESIGN

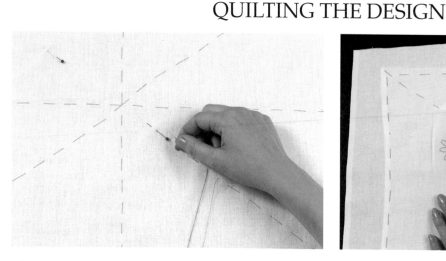

1 Lay the pillowcase front out flat, wrong side up. Center the muslin on top and pin it in place. Find the center of each edge, and baste to the center mark on the opposite edge both vertically and horizontally. Baste diagonally from corner to corner, and around the edges. Remove pins.

2 Transfer the daisy design given on page 74 to the right side of the pillowcase front, using a transfer pencil and following manufacturer's directions. Make sure it is at least 2" (5 cm) from the edges of the muslin, or it will be too close to the flange.

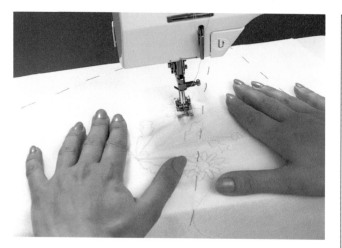

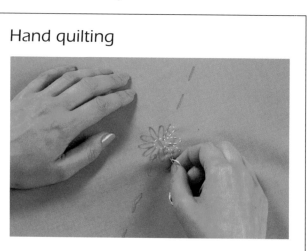

Hand quilting

3 Set your sewing machine to a medium-length stitch. Sew along the design lines; work slowly and carefully, using a continuous line of stitching as far as possible. Pull the thread ends to the wrong side, knot together and trim.

Thread a needle with sewing thread, quilting cotton or two strands of embroidery floss. Use tiny running stitches along the design lines, or backstitch, if you prefer. Use an embroidery hoop to prevent puckering.

4 Stuff the large areas of the design first. Use your scissors to cut a small slit in the muslin at the center of a large leaf. Cut along the grain, where possible. Pull apart a small amount of fiberfill; use tweezers, stylus or tapestry needle to insert it through the slit and stuff the area quite generously. When you are happy with the padding, whipstitch the gap closed with matching thread. Repeat for all the large areas of the design.

5 Stuff the smaller areas, such as the daisy petals. Use your toothpick, stylus or tapestry needle to separate the muslin threads in the center of each area to be stuffed. Insert the stuffing, a little at a time, as before. Ease the threads back after stuffing, and whipstitch, using matching thread.

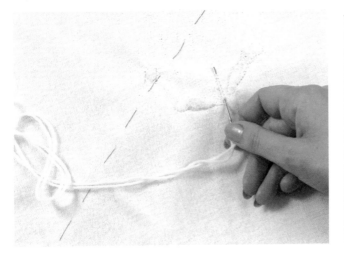

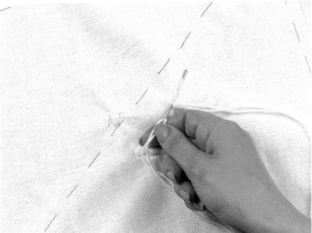

6 Thread a tapestry needle with yarn or soft cord, using a double length, if desired. Insert the needle at the starting point, separating the muslin threads, and run it along the channel for up to 1 1/4" (3.2 cm). Bring it out and pull to leave a short end of 1/4" to 3/8" (6 mm to 1 cm).

7 Reinsert the needle through the exit hole and thread it along the channel again, bringing it out as before. Repeat to fill the whole channel. Curves require bringing the needle out more often for a smooth fit. Use an embroidery hoop or stretch the fabric periodically to prevent puckering, making sure you hold onto the yarn or cord end. Snip off the yarn or cord to finish, again leaving a short end.

8 Turn your fabric over to see how the design is progressing on the right side at regular intervals. If you don't think you have added enough padding, insert some more by first separating the muslin threads as in step 5. To add more padding to the stems, just thread another length of yarn or cord as before, making sure you secure the original length so you don't push it out of place.

MAKING THE PILLOWCASE

1 Lay the lining fabric over the muslin on the back of the finished design; pin it in place across the center and around the edges. The lining is essential to protect the muslin from wearing against the pillow or being damaged in the wash.

2 Construct the pillowcase following the instructions on page 70. When the pillowcase back is in place, baste near the inner flange folds and remove the basting threads holding the quilting layers together. Finish the flange with a decorative stitch, if desired.

TRACE-OFF DAISY DESIGN

LOG CABIN PATCHWORK QUILT

Create an exquisite patchwork quilt to dress up your bed or display as a wall hanging. The popular log cabin design featured here is colorful, versatile and quick to sew.

Log cabin is one of the simplest and quickest forms of patchwork, so even a large project such as a quilt can be completed in a relatively short period of time. Strips are stitched around a central square, with their short ends overlapping in a steplike effect, to form square blocks. The blocks are then joined to make the quilt, which is framed with three rows of wide border strips. There are no time-consuming templates to deal with – all the fabric strips are cut to the same width, and trimmed to the correct length as they are stitched in place.

In traditional log cabin patchwork, strips of light-colored fabrics, symbolizing sunlit logs, are arranged on adjacent sides opposite strips of dark-colored fabrics, symbolizing shadowed logs. The central square represents the cabin hearth and is traditionally red to symbolize the fire – the heart of the home. Nowadays, a freer approach is often taken, and fabric designs and colors vary greatly.

The finished size of the log cabin quilt shown here is approximately 90" x 62" (229 x 158 cm). It is made of 15 square blocks, each one measuring 13¾" (35 cm) square, and three outer borders. To make a larger quilt, simply make more blocks and/or increase the size of the blocks by adding extra rows of strips.

For accurate results, use a rotary cutter and mat to cut out the strips, and be sure to sew exact ¼" (6 mm) seam allowances. Emphasize the log cabin design and secure the quilt layers together by stitching in the ditch; minimize the shifting of layers during quilt use by stitching along all the design lines.

When you stitch the individual patchwork blocks together to make your quilt, you can arrange them in a number of ways to create different patterns. On this dramatic quilt, the blocks are arranged in a 'fields and furrows' design, in which diagonal strips of light and dark are formed across the quilt, to resemble farmers' furrows. Traditional quilt books will show other options, some of which are shown on pages 79 and 80.

MAKING A LOG CABIN QUILT

YOU WILL NEED

- ➤ Closely woven cotton fabrics
- ➤ Cotton fabric for backing
- ➤ Mediumweight batting
- ➤ Rotary cutter, scissors
- ➤ Cutting mat
- ➤ Pins
- ➤ Matching sewing thread
- ➤ Safety pins (optional)

Measuring and cutting out

Center squares Cut fifteen 2½" (6.5 cm) squares

Patchwork strips Cut three strips 2½" (6.5 cm) wide across the width of each patchwork strip fabric, from selvage to selvage. Cut additional strips as you need them.

Outer borders Cut 6 strips, 3" (7.5 cm) wide from the first border fabric. Cut 8 strips, 4" (10 cm) wide from the second border fabric. Cut 8 strips, 5" (12.5 cm) wide from the third border fabric. Cut all the strips across the width of the fabric, from selvage to selvage.

Fabric requirements

Amounts are for a single quilt, 90" x 62" (229 x 157.5 cm), based on a fabric width of 44" (112 cm)

Patchwork blocks

Center square:	⅛ yd (0.15 m)
First light strip:	⅓ yd (0.32 m)
Second light strip:	½ yd (0.5 m)
Third light strip:	¾ yd (0.7 m)
First dark strip:	½ yd (0.5 m)
Second dark strip:	¾ yd (0.7 m)
Third dark strip:	1 yd (0.95 m)

Outer borders

First border (light fabric):	¾ yd (0.7 m)
Second border (mid-tone fabric):	1 yd (0.95 m)
Third border (dark fabric):	1⅜ yd (1.3 m)

Backing fabric 3¾ yd (3.45 m)

Batting 90" x 62" (229 x 157.5 cm)

MAKING A BLOCK, JOINING BLOCKS

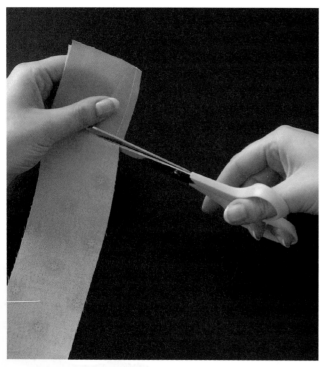

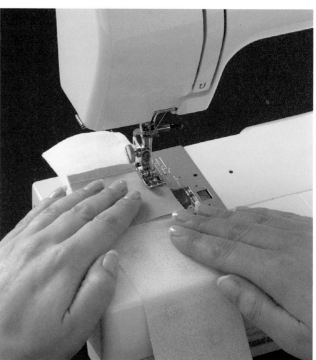

1 Pin the center square to the first light strip, right sides together and edges matching. Stitch ¼" (6 mm) seam allowance, using a stitch length of about 15 stitches per inch (2.5 cm). Trim the strip at the edge of the square; it is important to cut the strip at right angles to the long edges. Finger-press the seam allowance away from the center square.

2 Pin the same light strip to the edge of the center square/strip, right sides together, as shown. Stitch and trim the excess strip as in step 1. Finger-press the seam allowance away from the center.

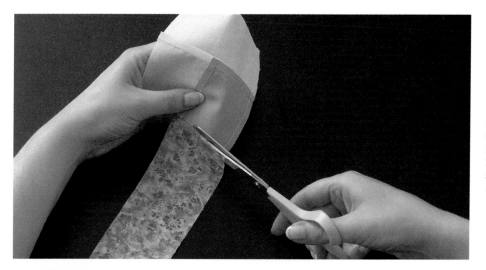

3 Pin the first dark strip to one side of the center section, as shown, right sides together. Stitch and trim as in step 1. Finger-press the seam allowance away from the center.

4 Align the same dark strip with the last edge of the center square, right sides together; pin, stitch, and trim the strip as in step 1, to make the block square. Press the seam allowance away from the center.

5 Begin the second round; take the second light strip and repeat step 1 to stitch the strip to the right-hand edge of the center section. Trim and finger-press as before.

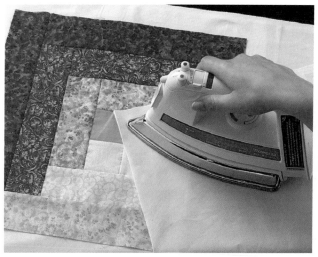

6 Complete the second round of the block; repeat steps 2 to 4 to add another second light strip, followed by two second dark strips. Press. Complete the block; add two third light strips, followed by two third dark strips, as in steps 1-4.

7 Press 15 completed blocks from the right side, using a pressing cloth. Arrange the blocks as desired. Stitch rows of blocks together, using 1/4" (6 mm) seam allowance; join rows, turning seam allowances in opposite directions. Press quilt top.

ADDING THE BORDERS AND BACKING

1 Measure width of quilt top (at center); trim two narrow, light border strips to this measurement. Align one trimmed border strip to the top edge, right sides together and raw edges matching; ease quilt top or border strip, if necessary. Pin and stitch, taking a ¼" (6 mm) seam allowance.

2 Pin and stitch the second trimmed border strip to the bottom edge of the quilt, right sides together and raw edges matching. Press seam allowances toward the quilt blocks.

3 Measure length of quilt top at center; join 2 sets of narrow border strips and trim to this measurement. Place one long border strip along one side edge of the quilt top, right sides together and raw edges matching. Pin and stitch, taking a ¼" (6 mm) seam; stitch across the ends of the top and bottom border strips.

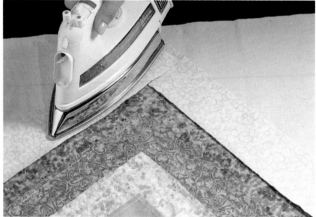

4 Complete the first border by stitching the second long border strip to the other side of the quilt top, taking ¼" (6 mm) seam allowance. Press the seam allowances toward the quilt blocks.

5 Repeat steps 1-4 to add two more borders; use the mid-tone fabric for the middle border, and the dark fabric for the outer border, and seam border strips as necessary to make the required length.

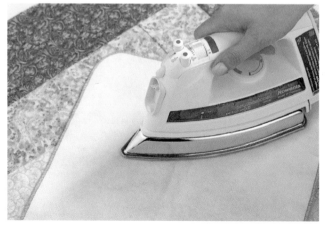

6 Press the border strips from the right side, using a pressing cloth.

ASSEMBLING THE QUILT

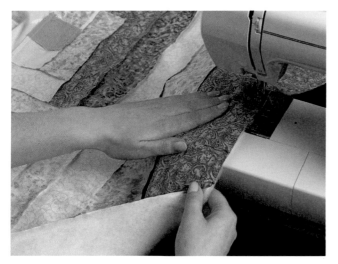

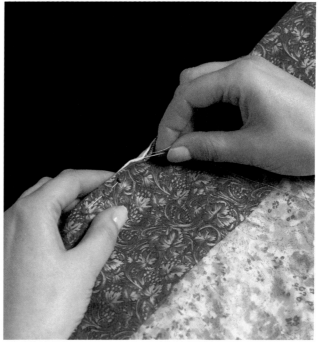

1 Cut batting to the same size as the quilt top, and lay it flat. Stitch widths of backing fabric together, as necessary, to make a piece the same size as the quilt top; lay it right side up over the batting. Smooth the layers. Place the quilt top right side down over the backing fabric; smooth. Pin the layers together. Stitch around the edges, taking a ¼" (6 mm) seam allowance; leave a 15" (38 cm) opening along the bottom; hold the layers firmly as you stitch to prevent them from shifting.

2 Turn the quilt right side out, making sure the corners are well pushed out. Turn in the edges of the opening; slipstitch closed.

3 Lay quilt flat. Baste layers together, using safety pins or long running stitches. Stitch in the ditch as desired, following the design lines of the quilt top; the design is quilted where the light and dark colors meet to enhance the zigzag pattern. Quilt by hand, if you prefer.

◄ *This quilt, made from a medley of pretty calicoes in blues, yellows and white, shows how your choice of fabrics and the way you arrange the blocks can create distinctive patterns.*

Heavier, richly textured fabrics, including soft wools and tweeds, brushed cottons and corduroys, have been combined to make this simple yet sumptuous quilt. Although it is made up from a wide assortments of fabrics, the quilt remains true to traditional log cabin design, with bright red central squares and a carefully balanced arrangement of light and dark fabric strips. Quilts made of wool or decorator fabrics must be dry-cleaned rather than washed.

The balance of light and dark fabrics and the arrangement of the blocks are crucial to the success of a log cabin quilt, so give them careful consideration before you begin. Note how, on this large bed quilt, the blocks are pieced together to form a pattern of dark and light diamonds.

This charming quilt is created from mix-and-match patchwork fabrics, which you can buy from specialty quilting stores. The blend of pretty mini-print calicoes in blue and white with a touch of pink gives the quilt fresh, country-cottage appeal.

APPLIQUÉ ANTIMACASSAR

Transform an armchair into a beautiful focal point for your room, with a richly textured appliqué antimacassar, in colorful and luxurious velvets, silks and satins.

Antimacassars were originally used to protect chair backs from hair styling oils (Macassar oils), popular in the nineteenth century. With a new twist, they can change the whole appearance of a chair or sofa and become exquisite home accessories in their own right.

The opulent antimacassar featured here is made from layered fabric motifs, appliquéd onto a background fabric and embellished with satin stitching. The design motif, inspired by peacock feathers, consists of a basic feather shape with two smaller 'eyes'. Templates for the design are given on page 84.

Choose elegant fabrics to make the antimacassar – velvets, silks and satins are ideal. Look through remnant bins in fabric stores, and hunt through your sewing box for leftovers from previous sewing projects. The background, onto which the shapes are fused and stitched, should be a stable, closely woven fabric – slubbed silk is used here, but you could opt for a less expensive alternative. You can make the lining from any fabric you wish; velvet is a good option, as its pile provides grip and prevents the antimacassar from shifting on the chair back. Always iron delicate fabrics using a press cloth or needle board.

The antimacassar shown here measures 17" x 38" (43 x 96.5 cm); larger versions make effective and sumptuous throws.

▲ *This appliqué antimacassar has been designed using a rich mix of greens, purples, pinks and blues, with a background fabric of dark green silk. You can use any color combination you wish, but make sure that there is sufficient contrast between the different elements of the design.*

MAKING AN APPLIQUÉD ANTIMACASSAR

Measuring and cutting out

Measure the width of your chair back, and add 2" (5 cm) for seam allowances. Decide how far down the front and back of the chair back you want the antimacassar to hang; measure between these points, over the chair back, and add 2" (5 cm) for seam allowances.

For the background Cut fabric to the above dimensions.

For the lining Cut fabric to the same dimensions.

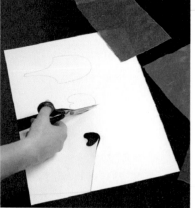

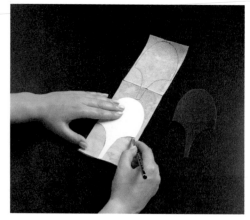

1 Fold the background in half lengthwise, and press a light crease down the center; this will serve as a guideline for positioning the feather motifs. Open the fabric, and use tailor's chalk to mark a 1" (2.5 cm) seam allowance all around the edges.

2 Trace the three templates on page 84 onto thin cards; cut them out. Decide roughly which fabrics will be used for each template; you may wish to use the same fabrics for all three templates, but combine them in different ways for each motif, as here.

3 Apply fusible web to the back of the fabrics you want to use for the main feather shapes. Draw around the largest template onto the backing paper, and cut out the shapes. Continue until you have an assortment of shapes to cover the background.

4 Lay the feather shapes right side up on the right side of the background, in the desired arrangement; center the first shape on the crease, 1½" (3.8 cm) from the top edge, and position shapes side by side until you reach the seamlines. Lay the next row of shapes below the first, overlapping them slightly and staggering the shapes so they fit into the arches formed by the lower edges of the first row. Continue until the entire background is covered. Shapes that overhang the edges will be trimmed later.

5 Repeat step 3, using the two remaining templates, to cut out one of each shape for each feather that lies fully on the background; there's no need to cut out shapes for feathers that overhang the sides of the background. Remove the paper from the back of the smallest motifs.

6 Center the small motifs on the medium-size motifs. Fuse to create the eyes of the feathers; use a press cloth or needle board to protect delicate fabrics. Remove the paper from the back of the eyes.

7 Stitch repeatedly around the raw edge of a small eye, using contrasting thread and straight stitch; cover the raw edge with the stitching. It doesn't matter if the stitching strays from the raw edge as this adds to the feathery effect. Repeat for the remaining feather eyes, using an assortment of contrasting threads.

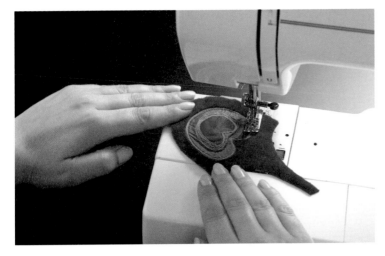

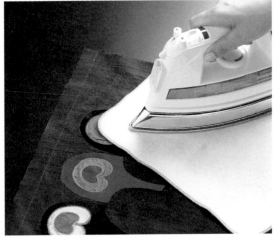

8 Arrange the eyes on the large feather shapes, except those that extend beyond the background. Move them around until you achieve a pleasing balance of colors and textures; each eye should lie about 1/2" (1.3 cm) from the curved end of the feather. Lift each feather in turn, and fuse the eye in place. Remove the back paper. Stitch around the outer edge of each eye, using a range of contrasting threads, as in step 7.

9 Fuse the first row of feathers in place on the background, using a press cloth or needle board. Position them carefully, with the first feather centered on the crease line, and all the feathers 1 1/2" (3.8 cm) from the upper raw edge.

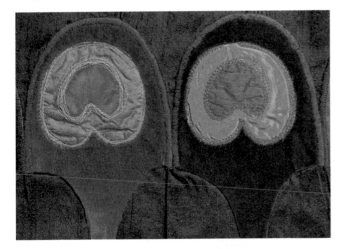

10 Stitch around the top arch of each feather in the first row, covering the raw edge with medium-width zigzag stitching; use an assortment of contrasting threads.

11 Fuse the next row of feathers into the arches formed by the first row. Overlap them slightly, so the raw edges of the first row are covered by the second. Fuse each feather in place; stitch as in step 10.

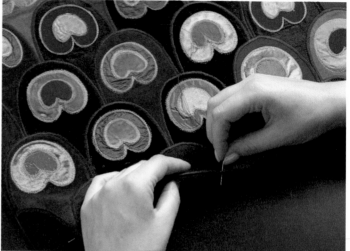

12 Repeat step 11 to fuse and stitch all the remaining rows of feathers. Use scissors to trim feathers extending beyond the edges of the background. Place the appliquéd fabric on the lining, right sides together and raw edges matching; pin. Machine-stitch around the antimacassar, using 1" (2.5 cm) seam allowance; leave 6" (15 cm) opening on lower edge. Trim the seam allowance and corners.

13 Turn the antimacassar right side out. Turn in the raw edges along the lower edge, and slipstitch closed. Press, using a press cloth and needle board.

You can display your finished antimacassar as a sumptuous wall hanging. Sew a fine fabric sleeve to the top and insert a length of dowel.

FEATHER TEMPLATE

Trace or photocopy the templates shown here to create the patterns for your peacock feather antimacassar.

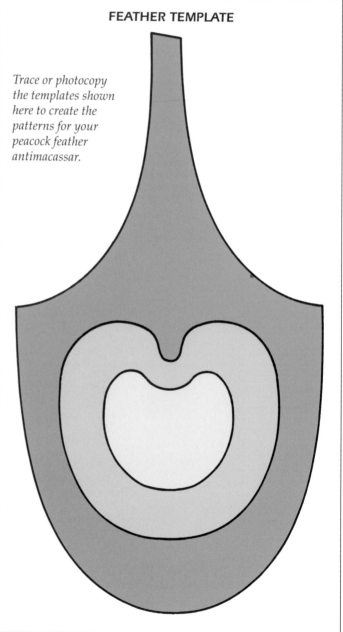

TRIANGULAR-POINTED VALANCE

Valances are an easy decorative option for windows. With minimum effort and only a small amount of fabric you can bring a plain window treatment to life.

A triangular-pointed valance makes a pretty border for a window when hung by itself, or it makes an attractive finishing touch when layered over curtains.

Generally, valances hang between one-sixth and one-eighth of the window height. The design of the triangular edge also depends on the window size and shape – choose between wide, shallow triangles or long, thin points. If you are unsure of how it will look, pin a sheet of paper or fabric remnant at the window and step back to gauge the length. Cut the lower edge into triangles to select the finished effect.

When you have decided on the proportions, draw a paper template the length of one fabric width. Use this to mark the design on the fabric.

Use decorator cottons in solids, florals and geometric patterns. Try to avoid large or complicated designs as these will swamp the window and be hard to match on a small area.

▲ *The check fabric used to make this pointed-edge valance provides a striking contrast to the soft billowing curtains. The checks determine the size of the triangular points – each point fits into one dark square of the pattern.*

MAKING A TRIANGULAR-POINTED VALANCE

Measuring and cutting out

Cut depth of valance Decide the valance depth at the longest point; add 2½" (6.5 cm) for seam allowances.

Number of fabric widths Measure the total length and return of the curtain rod and add 1" (2.5 cm) for side seams. Divide this measurement by the fabric width; round up to the nearest whole number. Allow 1" (2.5 cm) for sewing fabric widths together.

Quantity of fabric and lining Multiply the cut depth by the number of fabric widths; multiply the fabric repeat by the number of fabric widths, if matching a pattern at seamlines.

Cutting out Cut out the required number of valance depths from both fabric and lining across the fabric width. Trim off selvages.

MAKING THE TEMPLATE

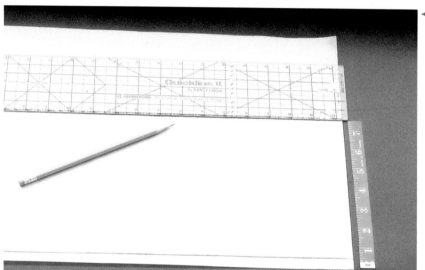

1 Cut a strip of paper the same width as the fabric width minus seam allowances and about 12" (30.5 cm) long. Mark two lines across the width of the strip ½" (1.3 cm) and 7½" (19.3 cm) from the lower edge.

2 Determine approximately how wide you want each triangle to be. Divide the total finished valance width by this measurement and round this figure up to the nearest whole number. Divide the valance width by this whole number to determine the exact width of the triangles.

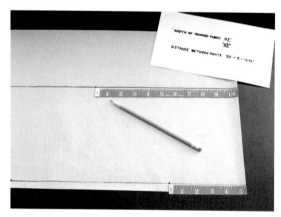

3 Mark points along the upper line that are spaced your determined triangle width apart. Mark points along the lower line spaced the same width apart, but starting and ending one half-width from each end.

4 Draw lines between the upper and lower points, forming a zigzag shape. Add ½" (1.3 cm) seam allowance along the lower edges of the template. Cut out the template along the marked seam allowance.

MAKING THE VALANCE

1 Join the fabric widths using ½" (1.3 cm) seams or matching pattern repeat. Repeat with the lining widths. Press seams open. Place the fabric on the lining, right sides together and raw edges aligned. Pin bottom of template along the lower edge of the fabric; place one end ½" (1.3 cm) from the raw edge and the other end on a seamline. Mark cutting line with a fabric marking pencil.

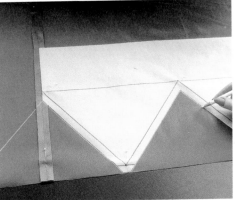

2 Remove and reposition the template along the length of the valance, placing template ends at the seamlines and even with the previously marked outline. Mark the shaped lower edge as before.

3 Continue marking the lower edge of the valance template to the end of the fabric, making sure there is a complete triangle and a ½" (1.3 cm) seam allowance at the end. Cut the fabric and lining along the chalk lines. Transfer the triangle points from the template to the fabric with a fabric marking pencil. Pin the fabric and lining together.

4 Stitch a ½" (1.3 cm) seam along the sides and lower edges of the valance, pivoting the fabric at the points. Trim the seam allowances at lower points and clip at upper points. Press the lining seam allowance toward the lining. Turn the valance right side out and press along the seamed edges.

5 Press under a 1" (2.5 cm) double hem on the upper edge of the valance, folding both fabric and lining together. Stitch close to the lower fold.

Hanging the valance

From a narrow curtain rod ➤
Machine-stitch a length of curtain heading tape to the wrong side of the valance, following the manufacturer's instructions. Insert curtain hooks through the tape to hang the valance.

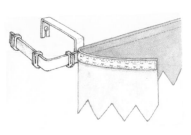

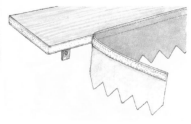

◄ On a mounting board
Machine-stitch a length of loop tape to the wrong side of the valance. Glue hook tape to the edge of the shelf. Simply press the two halves together to hang the valance.

Even a small window is enhanced by a pointed-edge valance. Created in the same fabric as the curtains, the points are left plain, giving the illusion of a wider window.

Emphasize the pendant effect of the pointed valance edges by decorating them with brightly colored beads, tassels or metallic charms.

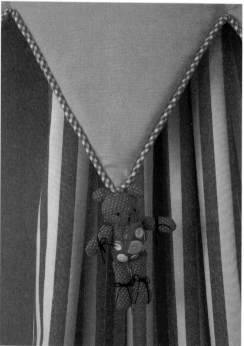

Quick touches add individuality to a child's room. This little polka-dot teddy is the perfect mascot to add to a valance and light enough to hang from each point. Buy or make an assortment of animals in cheery fabrics and hang them in a row.

ITALIAN-STRUNG CURTAINS

Use Italian stringing to give your curtains designer flair. Simply attach a system of cords and rings to the back of the curtains to create an elegantly draped effect.

Jane Churchill

Italian stringing is a technique that gives a graceful, feminine look to curtains. It uses a system of rings and cords, stitched and threaded to the back of the curtains, to pull them into soft folds and give the appearance of fuller, more luxurious drapes. The effect is similar to that achieved when using tiebacks, but because the curtains are gathered back at a higher point, they allow more light into the room.

The rings and cords are applied to finished curtains, so you can transform ready-made curtains or make your own. It works most effectively on lined or, better still, interlined curtains; unlined curtains are unlikely to have sufficient body to form sumptuous folds, and the rings and cords may show through to the front.

Italian stringing creates a formal look, so you'll find it works best with dressier heading styles, such as pencil or goblet pleats. Note that the style requires the heading to remain permanently drawn across the track. If you are making the curtains yourself, leave the heading ungathered until you have attached the rings for the Italian stringing.

▲ *Italian-strung curtains, drawn back high on the window, create a soft frame for an attractive view and give the impression of sumptuous drapes. With this style, the heading is the focal point as the sweep of fabric draws the eye upward. Neat, formal heading styles work best, such as the crisp pencil pleats used here.*

ADDING ITALIAN STRINGING

YOU WILL NEED

- ➤ Lined curtains to fit your window
- ➤ Matching sewing thread
- ➤ Masking tape
- ➤ Tape measure
- ➤ Air-erasable fabric marker, long ruler
- ➤ Scissors

- ➤ Curtain rings
- ➤ Nylon blind cord
- ➤ 1" x 2" (2.5 x 5 cm) wood batten, the length of the curtain track, and drywall screws
- ➤ 6 screw eyes
- ➤ Cleat

Plotting the curve

Attach one end of a tape measure to the center of the curtain track, using tape. Drape it to the side of the window, roughly one-quarter of the way down, to form the curve for the upper part of the curtain; note the curve measurement.

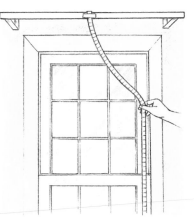

1 Lay the curtains right sides up, with the heading ungathered, if possible. Align the leading edges, and use a double thread to slipstitch them together, from the top edge to the bottom of the heading tape.

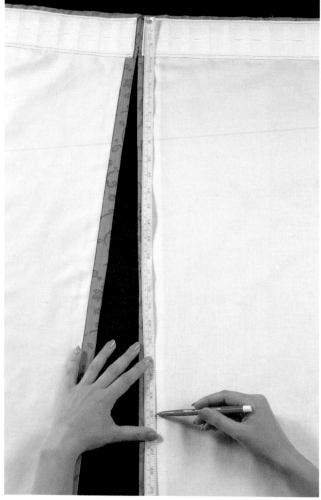

2 Turn the curtains over so they are lining sides up. Measure down from the curtain hook position on the heading tape the measurement taken in **Plotting the curve**, above. This should be about one-third of the way down the curtain. Use an air-erasable pen to mark this point on each leading edge of the curtain.

3 Mark a point about one-fifth to one-quarter of the way down the curtain on the outer edge of each curtain. Draw a straight diagonal line between the marks on each curtain panel, using an air-erasable pen; use a long ruler to help you mark a straight line.

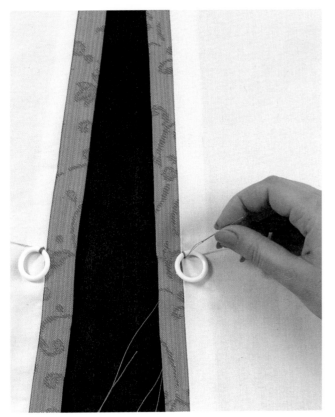

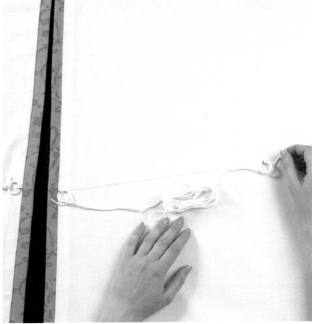

5 Tie a length of cord to the ring on the leading edge of each curtain, then run it through the other rings. Leave a long tail – you'll need enough to go up to the top, across the curtain again and halfway down the side.

4 Arrange rings at about 12" (30 cm) intervals along the marked lines, positioning one ring at each end and at least two in between; the finer your curtain fabric, the more rings you should use. Sew the rings in place through both the lining and main fabric, using thread to match the main fabric; keep your stitches small.

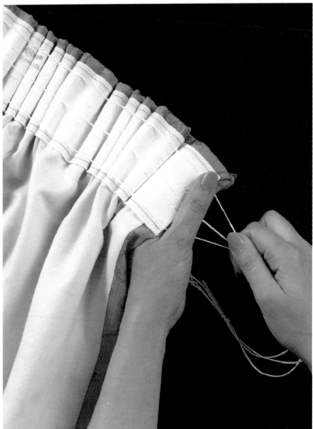

6 Attach the batten to the wall beneath the track, using screw (for illustration purposes, the batten is not shown on the wall). Insert screw eyes on the underside of the batten, one at center, one at one end, and two at the other end. Attach another screw eye to the wall or window frame at each side of the window, so they will be level with the outer rings on each curtain. On the side of the window with the double screw eyes, attach a cleat.

7 Pull the released gathering cords at the outer edges of each curtain to gather the headings to fit the track. Tie the cords in a neat bundle at the outer edges of the curtains. Hang the curtains in place on the track.

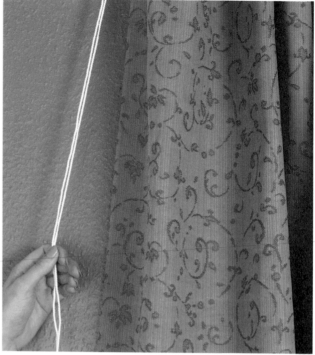

8 Slip each cord through the adjacent screw eye at the side of the window, and take it to the top of the window. For the curtain panel with two screw eyes at the top, pass the cord through both screw eyes and down to the cleat. Pass the other cord through all the screw eyes in the batten and down to the cleat.

9 Arrange the folds so the curtains gather evenly across the window. Pull the cords gently, until they are taut, but the curtains still hang straight. Knot the cords together below the cleat. Pull the cords to draw the curtains back from the window, and secure them on the cleat. Step back to check the effect. Arrange the folds.

◀ *Emphasize the lines of Italian-strung curtains by stitching a decorative trim along the leading edges. Here, the curtains are edged with scalloped fringe for a soft effect. They are lined with a coordinating decorator fabric for extra body.*

BEADED WINDOW BLIND

Make a feature of any window with this striking beaded blind. Sunlight shining through the bright beads will create a dazzling display of color to enliven your room.

This eye-catching window blind consists of two pieces of felt fused together. Cutout squares let the light in; each is embellished with a colored glass bead and edged with blanket stitches, using assorted colors of embroidery threads. The blind cannot be pulled up and down, so it is ideal for an overlooked window in a bathroom, or to screen an uninspiring view.

The blind is suspended from a dowel rod, enclosed in a felt casing. The instructions show how to hang the blind inside a window recess, but you can easily adapt them if you want to hang the blind on the outside. The

blind hangs inside the recess by means of screw eyes inserted into the dowel rod through the casing; the eyes are slipped onto cup hooks. To hang

▲ *Plain glass beads have been used for this blind, but for added sparkle, you could use cut glass beads instead. Embellish the edges of the cutout squares using different colored threads, with the colors arranged either randomly, as here, or to make a pattern.*

the blind outside the recess, cut the dowel slightly wider than the blind, and slip the ends into cup hooks attached to the wall or window frame at each side.

You can buy felt on the roll at fabric stores, and glass beads at craft or specialty stores.

MAKING A BEADED WINDOW BLIND

YOU WILL NEED

- Felt
- Scissors
- Paper-backed fusible web
- Metal ruler, pencil
- Craft knife and cutting mat
- Pearl cotton, in a variety of colors
- Pins

- Fine needle with a large eye
- Large glass or plastic transparent beads
- Tiny glass beads (optional)
- Wood dowel, ¾" (2 cm) in diameter
- Screw eyes and cup hooks

Measuring and cutting out

Main blind pieces Screw the cup hooks into the ceiling of the recess, and hang the screw eyes from them (see **Hanging the blind**, page 96, for details). Measure from the base of one screw eye to the windowsill, or to just above it; subtract 2¼" (6 cm) to allow for the dowel casing. Measure the width of the recess and subtract ¼" (6 mm). Cut two pieces of felt and one piece of fusible web to these dimensions.

Dowel casing Cut a piece of felt the same width as your blind, by 6" (15 cm) deep.

Dowel Cut a length of dowel the width of the blind minus ¼" (6 mm).

1 Fuse the paper-backed web onto one of the large felt pieces, so it is completely covered. Decide on the size and spacing of the cutout squares, and on the depth of the outer borders; consider the overall size of the blind and the size of your beads. Use a metal ruler and pencil to mark a grid of the desired dimensions on the backing paper; mark the squares to be cut out with a cross.

2 Lay the marked-up blind on a cutting mat. Cut out all the squares marked with a cross, using a craft knife and metal ruler.

3 Peel the backing paper from the felt, and fuse it to the second large felt piece; do not fuse approximately 2" (5 cm) at the top of the blind.

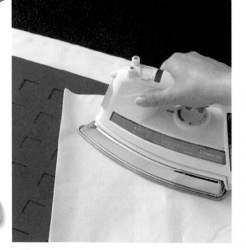

4 Anchor pearl cotton 2" (5 cm) from upper right corner of blind. Finish sides and bottom with blanket stitches; insert needle and bring it up over thread looped along edge. Work diagonal stitches at corners as on page 62, step 3. Stop 2" (5 cm) from upper left corner.

5 Lay the blind on a cutting mat. Use a craft knife to cut through the backing piece of felt, using the existing cutout squares as a guide, so that the squares become holes. Leave the top row of squares uncut.

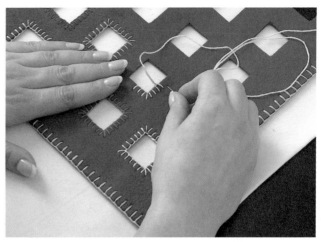

6 Work blanket stitches around the edges of each cut-out square, using pearl cotton in the colors of your choice. Conceal thread ends before trimming them.

7 Fold the piece of felt for the dowel casing in half lengthwise. Stitch the long edges together, using ½" (1.3 cm) seam allowance.

8 Lay the dowel casing along the open end of the blind, sandwiching the seam of the casing between the two felt pieces; align the stitching line just below the top of the blind. Pin along the top of the blind to hold the casing securely in place.

9 Work blanket stitches around the ends of the dowel casing, along the raw top edge of the blind, and down the sides to meet the existing blanket stitches; leave casing ends open. Repeat steps 5 and 6 to cut out and blanket-stitch the top row of squares.

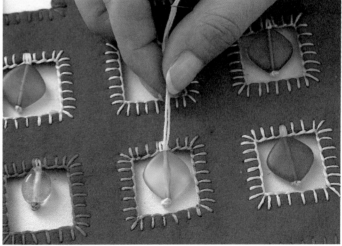

10 Secure pearl cotton or thread to the center top edge of one cutout square. Slip a bead onto the needle; slide it firmly against the felt. Knot the thread at the bottom of the bead to hold it in place. Take the thread back through the bead and secure it at the top; trim thread close. Repeat to stitch a bead to each square.

HANGING THE BLIND

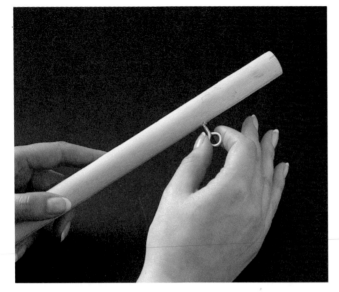

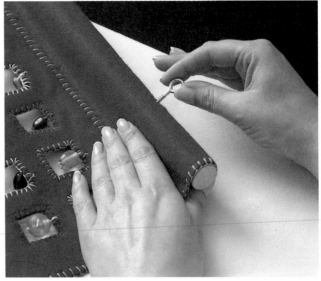

1 Screw two cup hooks into the ceiling of the window recess, about one-quarter of the way in from the sides; for a wide blind, add a third hook halfway across. Sand the ends of the dowel. Screw two – or three – screw eyes into the dowel to correspond with the positioning of the cup hooks. Remove screw eyes.

2 Insert the dowel into the dowel casing, so the screw eye holes lie along the top edge. Feel through the felt for the holes in the dowel, and insert the screw eyes, screwing them into place through the felt. Hang the blind in place by slipping the screw eyes onto the cup hooks.

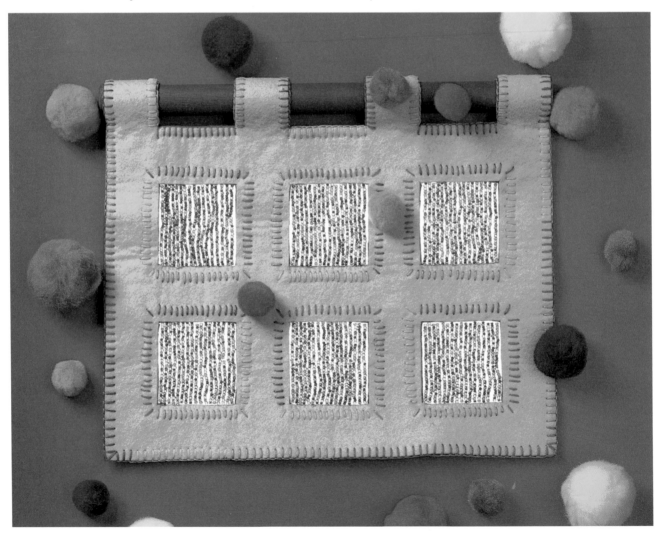

▲ *For a slight variation on the original blind design, thread tiny glass beads of different colors onto strands of nylon filament thread; secure at top and bottom edges of larger cutout squares. This creates a delicate texture for the sunlight to shine through.*

PAINTING ON SILK

Painting on silk enables you to create brilliant fabric designs, alive with color. Use the gutta resist method described here, or experiment with freehand silk painting.

Silk painting divides into resist and freehand techniques, each giving very different results. In the resist method featured here, gutta – a blocking solution – is used to outline each color area of the design and stop colors running into one another; the result is a clear, well-defined pattern. In freehand silk painting, the colors are allowed to merge and bleed into one another, giving an effect similar to a water-color painting.

You can buy silk paints, tubes or bottles of gutta, and other silk painting equipment, at art supply and specialty fiber stores. Gutta is available in transparent form, in which case it is generally washed out once the design has been set; or you can buy colored gutta in black, gold, silver and other metallic shades to add a permanent color to the design.

You start by using the gutta to trace the design onto the silk; if using a bottle of gutta, use a fine nib or nozzle to help you control the flow. The gutta dries and seals the fabric quite quickly. You can then fill in each color area, using an artist's brush and silk paints. Practice using the gutta on paper or scrap material before you begin to achieve a smooth, continuous flow, free of blobs.

▲ *Silk takes color extremely well, so it's easy to create vibrant effects. Here, the geometric design featured on the following pages has been made into a shallow seat cushion. A length of blue satin ribbon stitched around the edges adds a neat finishing detail and conceals the seam.*

SILK PAINTING USING GUTTA

- ➤ Large piece of paper, pencil and ruler
- ➤ Black marker pen
- ➤ Evenweave, smooth-surfaced silk, in white or cream
- ➤ Wooden frame, 3-point silk tacks
- ➤ Transparent gutta
- ➤ Fine gutta nib (optional)
- ➤ Artist's palette
- ➤ Water-based silk paints, in desired colors
- ➤ Good-quality artist's brush(es)
- ➤ Container of water
- ➤ Backing fabric, matching sewing thread and pillow form (optional)

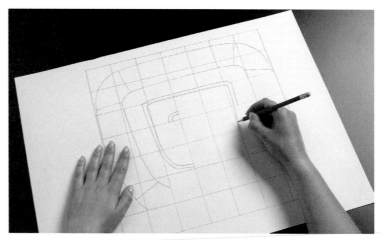

1 Enlarge the template on page 100 to the desired size, using the grid technique, shown above, or a copy machine. To create a cushion approximately 13¾" (35 cm) by 13" (33 cm), as featured here, you need to make each square on the grid 2" (5 cm).

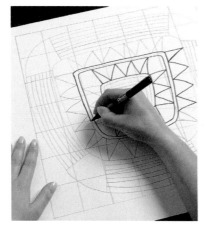

2 Carefully draw all the design lines using a black marker pen, so that you will be able to see them clearly through the silk.

3 Wash the silk in soapy water to remove any manufacturer's finish or grease, and rinse thoroughly. While the silk is still damp, lay it flat on a clean cloth, and press it well.

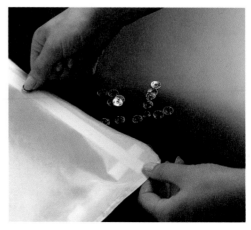

4 Lay the silk over the frame. Secure it at center of one side, using a silk tack. Stretch it to the opposite side and secure with a tack across from the first tack. Repeat to secure the silk at center of two remaining sides, keeping it taut.

5 Secure the silk all around the frame at regular intervals, working out toward the corners and keeping the silk taut. It is important that the silk is stretched tight across the frame, so that it won't sag when you paint it.

6 Place the enlarged design under the frame. Attach a fine gutta nib, if using a bottle of gutta, and trace along the design lines onto the silk. Work from the top to the bottom to avoid smudging, and keep your hand moving to achieve a smooth, continuous flow, free of blobs. Make sure that all the design lines are traced, and that there are no breaks for the paint to seep through.

7 Mix a palette of colors: use an artist's brush to transfer the silk paints onto the palette, mixing colors, if desired. Be sure to rinse the brush in water between colors to avoid contaminating one color with another. To create a tint, simply dilute paint with water.

8 Apply silk paint in your first chosen color to the design, using an artist's brush. Keep the brushstrokes light, and allow the paint to bleed from the brush to the gutta lines.

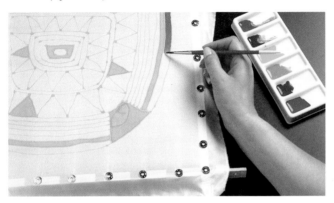

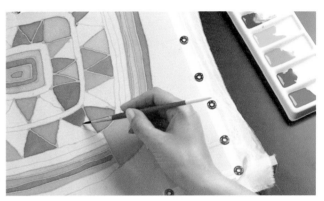

9 When you have completed all the areas of the design in the first color, clean the brush to avoid muddying the colors, or use a different brush for each color. Use the same technique as in step 8; the gutta lines act as a barrier, preventing the colors from bleeding into one another.

10 When you have completed all the areas in the second color, apply the third and subsequent colors, until the design is complete. If desired, paint a border around the outside of the design to enlarge it to the required size for your cushion pad. Allow to dry.

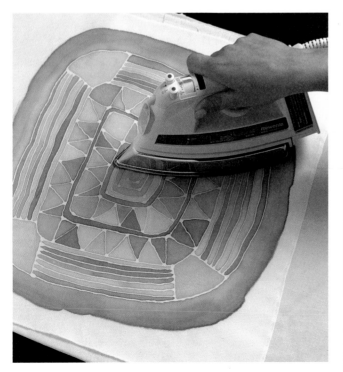

11 Carefully remove the silk from the frame. Set the silk paint colors, following the manufacturer's instructions.

12 Wash the finished design to remove the gutta. Press. To make a cushion, trim the design ⅝" (1.5 cm) beyond the painted outline; use silk as a template to cut backing fabric the same size. Place the fabric pieces right sides together, pin and stitch, taking a ⅝" (1.5 cm) seam and leaving an opening in the back edge. Turn right side out, insert the pillow form; slipstitch the opening closed.

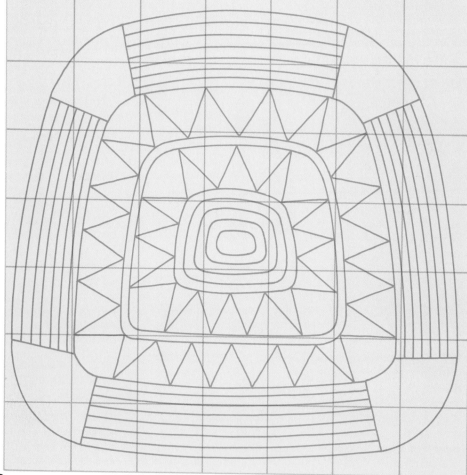

A floral design outlined in gold gutta and painted in bright, clear colors against a pale lavender background makes an exotic tray cloth. To add depth to the design, the petals are shaded in two colors: pink at the base merging into orange at the tips.

Hanging a painted silk panel at the window shows off the translucent quality of the paint colors and brings them to life. The design featured here is reminiscent of a stained glass window – black gutta is used, as well as transparent gutta, to give the impression of leading.

CUSHION DESIGN

Finishing Touches

Special decorative details may be used to enhance a particular decorating style or theme. Structural embellishments may be so simple they seem to be original architectural elements, or they may create a focal point in a room. Any piece of furniture or accessory may be finished to add interest or unexpected personal charm.

Consider adding an architectural molding to soften the line between your walls and ceiling. Install colorful tiles to highlight ordinary features and protect surfaces. Create colorful mosaics with crockery or paint. Apply a faux leopard skin finish to any paintable surface. Embellish basic terra-cotta pots with assorted clay shapes. Hang a delightful wind chime anywhere it can catch a breeze, or assemble a chalkboard for a message or play center. Cut special lampshades or make unique door knobs for striking details.

INSTALLING CORNICE MOLDING

*Cornice molding is the traditional
way of masking the transition between wall and ceiling,
adding character and decorative detail to a room.*

A room without a cornice can look unfinished, especially in a period home. Whether you favor ornate, highly decorative styles or simple, streamlined molding, you're sure to find a style to suit your taste, room decor and budget. Most home improvement centers stock an extensive choice of moldings in a variety of materials, including wood, plaster, plastic and polystyrene.

Depending on the type of molding you choose, and its weight, installation methods vary. The instructions show how to put up plain concave molding – a popular choice for modern homes where a clean, uncluttered look is preferred. The molding shown here is similar in construction to plasterboard, so is lightweight and easy to handle – though you will find an extra pair of hands helpful. Most plastic moldings are also simply glued in place, but wood moldings need finishing nails and heavier plaster moldings need screws.

Tubed adhesives are easily applied using a mastic, or caulk, gun. They

It's important to choose molding that suits the scale and style of the room. Plain molding, shown here, is a simple style that suits most settings.

dry quickly and have sufficient 'grab' that short lengths of molding need to be held in position for only a few moments. Longer sections may need to be lightly nailed or supported for an hour or so with softwood props, padded and wedged between the molding and the floor at an angle.

Before you start

Estimating quantities Find out in what standard lengths your chosen molding is available, and whether pre-formed corners or blocks (see page 106) are available. Measure each wall to determine how many lengths you need. Add an extra 6" (15 cm) to each length that ends in a corner to allow for the miter joint, plus an extra half-length for safety.

Preparing the walls Remove wallcovering from the wall and ceiling surface between the molding guidelines (see **Marking the walls**, steps 1 and 2, below) or the molding may pull any poorly applied wallcoverings away.

YOU WILL NEED

➤ Molding
➤ Strong adhesive
➤ Tape measure
➤ Timber or straightedge
➤ Pencil
➤ Fine-toothed tenon saw

➤ Miter box
➤ Putty knife
➤ Stepladder
➤ Temporary timber props and padding
➤ Spackle

MARKING THE WALLS

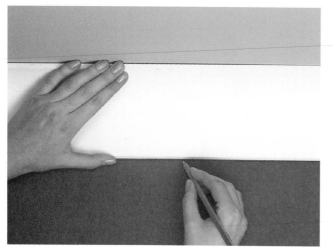

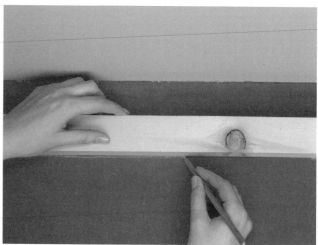

1 Cut a short length of molding to use as a template for marking guidelines on the walls. Most molding manufacturers stamp 'top' and 'wall' onto the flat rear surfaces of each molding length – position these surfaces against the appropriate area and, working around the room, make a small pencil mark at intervals.

2 Join all the marks around the room, using a length of timber or straightedge. These lines will act as a guide to ensure that you secure successive lengths of molding in place accurately.

CUTTING AND SECURING

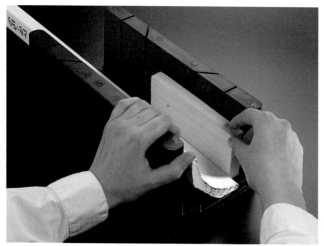

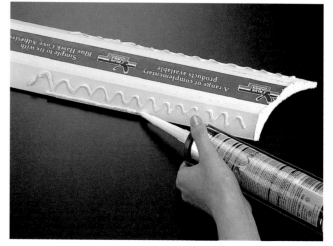

1 Cut an internal corner miter on one end of the first length of molding (see **Trouble-free miters**, opposite). Place the molding in the miter box; it's important that the molding sits squarely in the box so that the miters can be cut correctly. With one edge of the molding held flat against the side of the miter box, pack the space with scrap timber to prevent it from slipping while sawing. Cut an identical miter at the other end of the molding for joining to the next piece.

2 Squeeze adhesive onto the flat surfaces that will come into contact with the wall and ceiling. Finish with a line of adhesive along each edge. Fix to the wall with the pencil line as a guide, 'top' and 'wall' edges in the correct position. Press the molding gently but firmly – the adhesive will squeeze out. Hold or prop in position, then allow to dry for several minutes. Before the adhesive has set completely, cut away any excess with the putty knife for a neat, smooth finish.

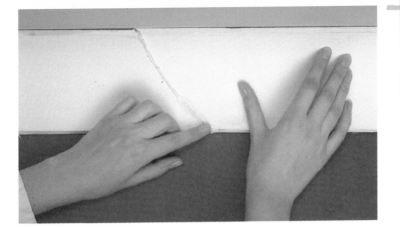

Trouble-free miters

● Cutting *molding* miters can be tricky. There are both left and right-hand miters for internal corners, and left and right-hand miters for external corners. The best way of avoiding costly mistakes (mitering the wrong angle on a complete length of molding, for example) is to mark the direction of the miter on each length of molding – make a pencil mark at the top and bottom every time. For extra safety, you can make a series of practice cuts on a spare length of molding, which you can then assemble to form the required miters.

● For corners other than right angles, such as a window bay, you will have to cut the molding without the aid of a miter box. Manufacturers or suppliers will advise, so ask when you buy.

3 Hold up the next length of molding and mark according to the required miters. (Take care to mark the direction of the miter on the molding every time – see **Trouble-free miters**, right.) Lengths on a flat wall should be joined using a miter join as shown, where one internal miter meets one external miter. Cut the molding, check the fit, apply the adhesive and hold or prop in position. When dry, run a finger full of spackle into the join for a perfect finish.

ALCOVE AND CHIMNEY CORNERS

1 When you reach the chimney breast wall, fit the section of molding along the rear wall of each alcove first; measure the length of the pencil line in the alcove, transfer the measurement to the base of a length of molding, then cut two internal miters – one for the left and one for the right. Apply the adhesive, then position the molding. Repeat for the right-hand alcove.

2 Next, fix the molding to the front of the chimney breast. Mark the molding length against the breast itself, then cut a left-hand and right-hand external miter on each end. Apply the adhesive and fix into position.

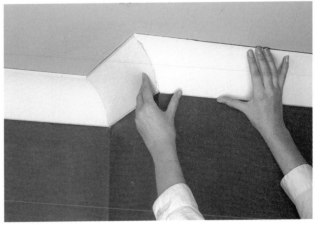

3 Hold up a short length of molding to each of the chimney breast sides. Mark the required length at the base, then cut two miters on each – an internal and external corner for the left and right-hand side. (The sections should resemble a parallelogram when cut.)

4 Check the fit of each mitered section, apply adhesive and fix in place as before. Fill any small gaps, if necessary, with a finger full of spackle. When you are satisfied that all the molding is dry, remove any props and paint, using standard paint in the color of your choice.

► *For rooms that require more decorative detail, cornicing is available with relief molding. Ceiling roses, dado rails and panel moldings are often available to match.*

▼ *Cornicing with patterned detail should be matched on visible points, such as alcove or chimney corners, wherever possible.*

Corner blocks

Some molding manufacturers offer matching pre-formed corner pieces or blocks, which are designed to butt-join lengths of cornice and eliminate the

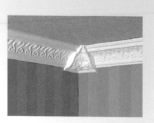

need for mitered corners. Both internal (top) and external (bottom) corner pieces are available. Secure the corner blocks before the lengths of molding.

► *If you have high ceilings in your home, choose cornicing to match the scale of the room. Deep cornicing with relief molding is available in a variety of designs.*

TILING A BACKSPLASH

Tiling a backsplash on the wall above a sink or basin gives you the perfect opportunity to try simple tiling skills. The result is a surface that looks good and is practical and hardwearing.

▲ *Create a simple backsplash with one row of plain tiles and one row of delicately patterned tiles that blend gently with the soft tones of the bathroom.*

If you are new to tiling, a backsplash makes an ideal first project because there is only a small area to cover and rarely any need to cut out difficult shapes. With the help of a few basic tools and materials, it is a simple and satisfying job.

To be sure that your tiles look good and stay in place, you must first prepare the wall so it is as clean and even as possible. You can secure tiles onto paint and plaster, and even onto old tiles, but not onto paper and other wallcoverings, so always remove these first.

After preparing the wall, determine how you are going to position the tiles. For a balanced look, center the tiles along the back of the basin, so there's a tile each side of the centerpoint or the middle tile lies over the centerpoint. Set the first row of tiles against the basin if its rim is straight and level, or use strip lumber to support the upper rows of tiles and cut tiles to fit around the basin later.

TILING A BACKSPLASH

YOU WILL NEED

- ➤ Tiles
- ➤ Carpenter's level
- ➤ Strip lumber, hammer and nails (optional)
- ➤ Tile adhesive and adhesive spreader
- ➤ Tile spacers
- ➤ Cloths and sponges
- ➤ Tile cutter and file (optional)
- ➤ Tile grout and flexible spreader
- ➤ Grout joint finisher
- ➤ Tub and tile caulk

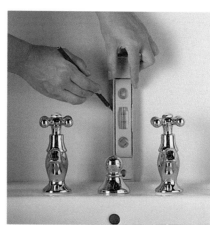

1 Measure and mark the center back edge of the basin or sink. Use a carpenter's level to draw a vertical line on the wall at this mark. Decide whether you want to position the middle tiles either side of the vertical line or centered over the vertical line.

2 Apply tile adhesive to the wall, using an adhesive spreader; draw the notched side of the spreader across the adhesive to give a combed effect with an even coverage. Apply enough adhesive to position all the tiles in the first row. Make sure you can still see the vertical line.

3 Place the first tile in position on the wall, aligning one edge or the middle of the tile with the vertical guideline, depending on the tile arrangement you prefer. The lower edge of the tile should be one grouting space above the basin rim, or flush with the strip lumber, if the basin is shaped. Press the tile firmly into place.

4 Fit tile spacers into the adhesive at all four corners of the first tile. Position the second tile adjacent to the first; continue spacing and securing the tiles along the row. Wipe off any excess adhesive.

Tiling above a shaped-rim basin

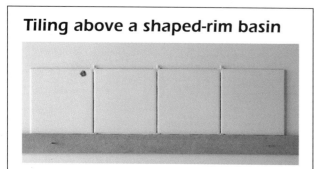

Measure one tile height plus one grouting space above the lowest point of the basin rim. Use a carpenter's level to mark a horizontal line at this height. Nail strip lumber to the wall so its top edge is level with the horizontal line, hammering the nails only partway in. Tile above the strip, following steps 1-4. Make sure the tiles are flush with each other and adjust if necessary. Carefully remove the strip. Cut and secure tiles to fit around the basin rim (see **Cutting and shaping tiles**, opposite). Finish, following steps 6-8.

5 Check that the tiles are flush with each other. Press in any tiles that are sticking out. Lift out any that have sunk in too far, and spread more tile adhesive on the wall before repositioning them. Apply more tile adhesive and continue tiling to complete the backsplash.

6 Allow the adhesive to dry for 12-24 hours. Load a small amount of grout onto the flexible spreader and draw it across the tiles, forcing the grout into the spaces between the tiles. Use a damp sponge to wipe off any surplus grout.

7 When the grout begins to harden, smooth along the joints with a joint finisher or narrow piece of dowel. This removes any excess grout and leaves the surface slightly concave. Wipe off any remaining grout and then polish the surface with a dry cloth.

Cutting and shaping tiles

To cut and shape tiles, you will need a straightedge, a tile cutter, tile nippers and a tile file. Try not to cut tiles to less than one-third their original width, as they may crack.

Measure the gap to be filled and mark on the tile with a grease pencil, allowing for the grouting space.

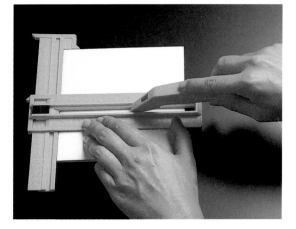

Straight cuts Score along the marked line using a straightedge and tile cutter. Snap the tile using a device in the cutter handle or by placing the tile on a matchstick and pressing on either side of the line. Alternatively, use a combination cutting tool.

Shaped cuts Mark the tile and score along the line with a tile scribe/cutter. Use pincers or tile nippers to snap off the waste a piece at a time. Smooth the cut edges with a tile file.

8 Seal the space between the tiles and basin using tub and tile caulk. Apply caulk with an even pressure and push the tube away from you along the space. Dampen your finger and smooth the caulk lightly. Allow it to set; trim off any excess caulk with a sharp blade.

▲ Add a lively splash of color to a wall and shelf with these brightly patterned handmade tiles.

▲ Here, an attractive shell-patterned backsplash extends to the sink surround, providing an ideal waterproof surface for bath accessories.

▶ Finish off a plain white backsplash with black-and-white-patterned border tiles to add understated contemporary elegance to a bathroom.

CROCKERY MOSAICS

The art of mosaic can transform a plain, utilitarian vase into a dramatic piece of artwork. Create your own mosaic masterpiece using colorful broken crockery.

Crockery mosaic is perfect for embellishing small decorative items such as mirrors, picture frames, boxes, wall plaques and flowerpots. In fact, you can use mosaic on almost any surface that is clean, dry and structurally sound.

Garage sales and second-hand stores are good hunting grounds for inexpensive, mismatched or damaged crockery. Try to select pieces with a particular color scheme in mind, because one or two shades are often more effective than using every color in the rainbow.

You may be inspired to create a mosaic on a theme by using only spotted or floral crockery, for example. If possible, collect crockery with all-over colors or patterns that will yield lots of colorful mosaic pieces when broken up. If you are using ceramic pieces that are irregularly shaped, from a broken teacup, for example, avoid using them on a totally flat surface, such as a table.

The basic technique is very straightforward – fragments of crockery are glued to a rigid background with tile adhesive, and the gaps between them are filled with tiling grout. If you use waterproof adhesive and grout, you can display the mosaic item outdoors. If necessary, the crockery pieces can be shaped using tile nippers that are available at home improvement centers.

Personal safety is important. Wear safety goggles when breaking or cutting the crockery to protect your eyes from any flying shards. When using the tile nippers, you may want to cut the pieces inside a paper bag as a safety precaution. Wear rubber gloves when applying adhesive and grout, since it can be irritating to the skin.

◄ *Crockery mosaic can give a colorful makeover to all sorts of household items. Here, an old vase is given a new lease on life – covered with a random arrangement of pretty broken china pieces.*

MAKING A MOSAIC POT

YOU WILL NEED

- ➤ Terra-cotta flowerpot or other item for decorating
- ➤ Old crockery
- ➤ Thick cloth or sack
- ➤ Safety goggles
- ➤ Hammer or mallet

- ➤ Tile nippers
- ➤ Ceramic tile adhesive
- ➤ Ceramic tile grout
- ➤ Old knife
- ➤ Grout spreader
- ➤ Sponge

Mosaic design

If you want to create a pattern with the crockery mosaic, use poster putty to arrange the pieces temporarily as you create your design. Then remove the pieces one by one and lay them in the same arrangement on the work surface.

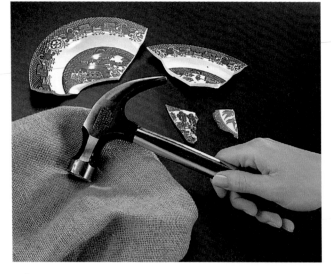

1 Break a few pieces of crockery at a time, keeping different colors or patterns separate. Wrap items in a thick cloth. Wearing safety goggles, hit the bundle with a hammer or mallet to break the items into pieces. Break large fragments into smaller ones in the same way.

2 If you want to cut shapes or fill in any gaps, use tile nippers or pincers to trim the broken crockery. Insert a piece of crockery into the nippers, aligning the blade with the required cut. Hold the nippers near the end of the handles and squeeze the handles together.

3 Using an old knife or a grout spreader, apply tile adhesive generously over a small section of the surface.

4 Press the crockery pieces firmly into the tile adhesive. The adhesive takes about 20 minutes to set, so you can reposition pieces if necessary. Continue applying adhesive and arranging the crockery pieces until the mosaic is finished. Allow it to dry for 24 hours.

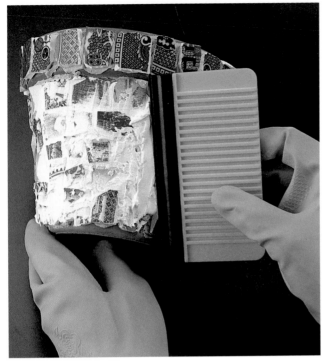

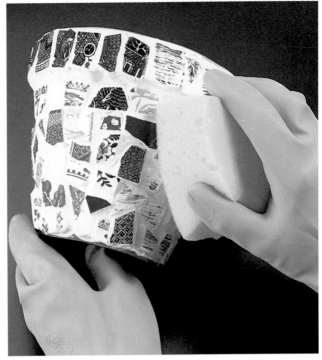

5 Apply a thick layer of grout over the mosaic, using the grout spreader. Take care to press the grout into the spaces between the crockery pieces.

6 Wipe off any excess grout with a damp sponge. Use an old knife to press extra grout into any gaps. Allow to dry, and wipe the surface again to give it a shine.

▼ *Blue and white china, interspersed with fragments of pink and green, transforms these plain terra-cotta flowerpots. Depending on how many fragments you have, you can extend the mosaic design over the entire pot, or just apply it to the rim.*

▼ Mosaic makes a colorful addition to a garden or patio. To decorate a tabletop, use flat pieces of crockery from a dinner or serving plate, or you could use broken ceramic tiles.

▲ China saucers with a pretty, all-over blue and white design, make up the mosaic on this charming picture frame. Use an inexpensive wooden frame as the base.

▲ For an interesting contrast, you could color the grout. Green artist's acrylic paint has been mixed into the grout before being spread over a mosaic planter.

▼ Single-color mosaics are very effective against the grout background. When you are decorating a curved surface, make use of curved crockery, such as a teacup or cereal bowl.

114

FAUX MOROCCAN TILES

Use spackle, paint and a stencil to create this exotic and colorful Moroccan tile effect, on walls, furniture and accessories.

Create a convincingly real handmade tile effect by applying a thick spackle and acrylic paint compound through a stencil plate. In the project on the following pages, faux tiles are applied to a tabletop. The pattern for the tiles is based on a historic Moroccan tile design.

The template is the key to the stencil. It is the smallest repeatable element to which the stencil can be reduced. It can be enlarged and repeated to create a stencil plate of the size required. A repetitious pattern is held together by 'ties' that connect the elements of the pattern. In this project the ties correspond with the grouting lines. A stencil based on this tracery of lines would be too frail, so the stencil has been divided into two stencil plates. You can use the template on page 118 to create the two stencils required for the project.

▲ *Glorious colors and a design derived from Islamic art are combined in this faux tiled tabletop. Created from a mixture of paint and spackle, these 'tiles' provide a highly decorative surface at very little cost.*

The tabletop used for this project is circular, but the pattern will also work on a rectangular surface. When preparing the stencils, start in the center of the surface and work outward to cover the required area. The tiling paste is made from spackle, which is available in powder form at home improvement centers. It is mixed with acrylic paint and applied to the stencil with a trowel. The stencil is removed and the mixture is left to dry for up to 12 hours, depending on the conditions.

TILED TABLETOP USING TEXTURE COMPOUND

YOU WILL NEED

- ➤ Template on page 118
- ➤ Tracing paper
- ➤ Fineliner pen
- ➤ Sharp craft knife and cutting mat
- ➤ Masking tape

- ➤ Transparent Mylar®
- ➤ Spackle, powder form
- ➤ Acrylic paint in white, red, yellow, blue and tan
- ➤ Plasterer's trowel

- ➤ Sandpaper, medium grade
- ➤ Polyurethane varnish, paintbrush
- ➤ Putty knife
- ➤ Sponge

From pattern to stencil

The diagrams below clearly show how the template and stencils A and B relate to the original table design. You will find this very helpful when you are doing the project, but refer to the steps for more details on creating the pattern.

The design The stencil pattern used to decorate the tabletop is derived from a Moroccan tile pattern. The diagram above shows the colorway of the design and is a useful guide when using the two stencil plates.

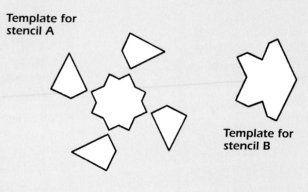

Template for stencil A

Template for stencil B

The design template This simple motif is the basic unit of the entire stencil and is repeated to form stencil plate A and, in turn, B. Use the gridded template on page 118 to make your template the required size.

Stencil plate A This is made by tracing the design template onto a sheet of transparent Mylar. The motif is repeated to form the whole stencil design. See **Creating the stencil**, step 1 for more information.

Stencil plate B This is made by outlining the shapes between the motifs traced onto stencil plate A, as shown in **Creating the stencil**, steps 2-4. The areas between the two shapes form the 'grouting' lines.

CREATING THE STENCIL

1 Enlarge the template on page 118 to an appropriate 'tile' size. Lay the enlarged pattern on a cutting mat and cut out the motif with a sharp craft knife.

Tape the template in the center of a sheet of transparent Mylar; trace the motif with a fineliner. Turn the template over, align it with one of the previously drawn quadrangles and tape it in place; trace around the motif again. Lift and rotate the template to align with the next quadrangle, and trace the motif again. Continue in this way to make stencil plate A.

2 Lay the Mylar on a cutting mat; cut out stencil plate A using a craft knife. Lay stencil A over a second sheet of tracing paper, tape both in position and trace the motifs. Remove stencil A.

3 Tape a second sheet of Mylar over the paper marked with stencil A. Draw a line approximately 1/4" (6 mm) inside one of the spaces between the motifs outlined in step 2, using a fineliner. The space between the motifs will form the 'grouting' line between the tiles.

4 Cut out the palmette shape marked in step 3 and use it as a template to mark the rest of stencil plate B; lay it centrally in the 'spaces' and draw around it to leave a 1/4" (6 mm) space all around. Cut out the shapes you have just marked, using a craft knife, to make stencil B.

CREATING THE FAUX TILES

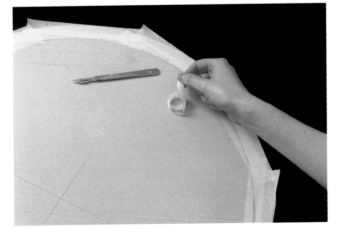

1 If you want to have a border around the 'tiles', mark the desired border width at the edge of the surface. Mask off the marked border using masking tape; on a round surface use the craft knife to trim the tape so that it follows the curved inner edge of the border.

2 Position stencil A on the surface and tape it in place. Mix four parts spackle to one part white paint. Add water until the mixture forms peaks. Apply the mixture generously to the stencil, using a trowel and spreading the mixture across every opening. Lift off the stencil plate and allow to dry.

3 Rub the surface lightly when it has dried thoroughly, using medium-grade sandpaper. Do not sand the surface too smooth.

4 Place stencil plate B on the surface, using the previously stenciled 'tiles' as a positioning guide. Secure the stencil in place with tape. Mix red, yellow and blue paint with spackle in three separate pots (see step 2). Apply the colored compounds through the openings of the stencil with a trowel, using the color guide on page 116. Lift off the stencil and allow to dry.

5 Sand the surface to remove any sharp peaks and ridges. Apply a simple stenciled border, if desired. Apply two coats of polyurethane varnish to the surface, allowing it to dry between coats. Allow to dry thoroughly.

6 Mix spackle and tan paint with water to create 'grout'; the mixture should have a fairly stiff consistency. Apply the 'grout' to the surface with a putty knife. Wash off the surplus with a damp sponge. Apply two more coats of varnish, allowing it to dry between coats.

▶ *This simple template is all you need to form stencil A and, in turn, stencil B. Before you start creating the stencil, you need to enlarge the template to an appropriate 'tile' size. Use either a photocopier or a grid to enlarge it.*

TILE DESIGN

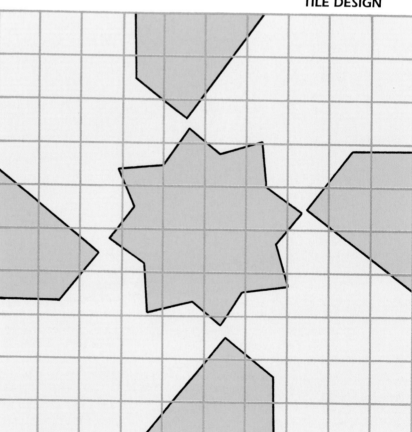

FAUX LEOPARD PRINT

*Add a touch of glamour to your home with
the golden tones and dappled patterns of leopard skin,
rendered with skill and style in oil paint.*

With their bold, abstract qualities and their glamorous associations, animal prints are a popular design motif and are surprisingly easy to replicate in paint. On the following pages you will find simple-to-follow instructions on re-creating the dappled patterns of leopard skin.

The success of the technique depends on observation. Note, for example, that on a leopard the dappling is not evenly distributed over the skin but lies in broad bands that flow along the animal's body. The fur beneath the dappling is darker in tone than the bands between. It's not necessary to reproduce the pattern exactly; it's more important to create an effect pleasing to the eye.

Like many paint techniques, faux animal patterns involve a basic two-step process – you apply the color, then soften the effect with a blending brush. For convincing results, apply the paint in the direction in which the fur lies, so that the brushmarks suggest animal hair. The pattern has been created with oil-based paint because it stays 'open' longer than acrylic, permitting you to soften the glazes and create subtle effects.

▲ *An ordinary bedside cabinet has been given a new lease on life with a leopard print makeover. The bold patterns and warm colors have a funky feel that suits this restrained contemporary interior, but would look equally at home in more dramatic surroundings.*

119

CREATING A LEOPARD PRINT EFFECT

YOU WILL NEED

- ➤ Latex primer, white
- ➤ Acrylic eggshell, white
- ➤ Artist's acrylic paint, in yellow ochre
- ➤ Saucer for mixing paint
- ➤ Paintbrushes, 2" (5 cm) and 1" (2.5 cm)
- ➤ Linseed oil, mineral spirits
- ➤ Small jar

- ➤ Palette for mixing paint
- ➤ Oil paint, in raw sienna, burnt sienna, yellow ochre, Van Dyke brown
- ➤ Artist's soft bristle brushes, round, nos.12 and 14
- ➤ Blending brush
- ➤ Piece of cloth
- ➤ Polyurethane varnish

1 Make sure the surface is clean and dust free. Use a 2" (5 cm) ➤ paintbrush to apply the white latex primer to the surface. Allow to dry. Apply the white paint to the surface. Allow to dry.

2 Mix a tiny amount of acrylic yellow ochre paint with the eggshell paint in a saucer to create a pale cream basecoat. Apply the color to the surface with a paintbrush.

3 Blend one part linseed oil with one part mineral spirits in a small jar; this is the medium for all your glazes. Put a dab of yellow ochre oil paint on a palette and add a drop of the glaze medium; blend the paint and the medium together. Apply the glaze where you want the darker, dappled bands of color to run, using sweeping strokes with the 1" (2.5 cm) brush; run out at an angle from the center of the band, and follow the growth patterns of the hair. Allow to dry.

Print reference

Study as many references as you can, including books on wildlife. Remember you are 'borrowing' a pattern rather than creating a zoologically correct illustration, so leopard print textiles (such as the fabric on the left) are often more helpful to use as a reference because the designer has already simplified the forms.

4 Add a little more yellow ochre to the glaze on your palette to create a slightly darker tone. Use the same 1" (2.5 cm) brush to lay another layer of color over the bands laid down in step 3. Follow the growth patterns as before, but make more emphatic brushmarks. This combination of light and dark tones will give depth to the hair. Allow to dry.

5 Put a small dab of burnt sienna and raw sienna on your palette, add a drop of the glaze medium, and mix. Place dots randomly within the band of darker tone, using a no. 14 brush; vary the size and shape of the dots.

6 While the paint is still wet, soften the spots with a blending brush. Drag the tip of the brush across the surface in the direction of the previous strokes. This elongates the spots and gives them a streaky appearance that emulates hair. Wipe the blending brush on a piece of cloth.

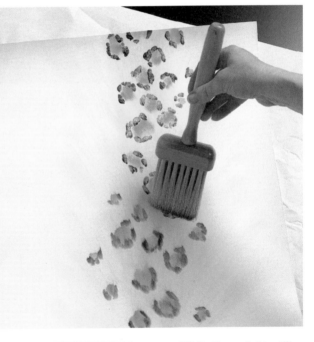

7 Put a dab of Van Dyke brown into your palette and add a drop of the glaze medium to thin it. Load the no. 12 brush with the glaze and lay a series of dashed marks in a U-shape around each spot.

8 While the paint is still wet, soften the spots with a blending brush, working in the direction in which the hair lies, as in step 6. Wipe the blending brush on a piece of cloth.

9 Divide the area between the band of spots in two and, using the no. 12 brush, lay dashes and dabs of paint that converge on this central line. Lay similar marks on the outside of the dabbled band.

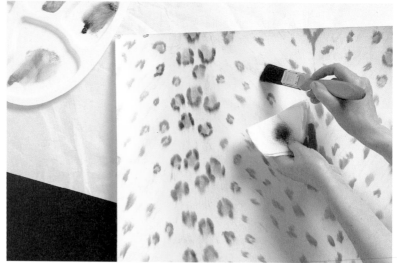

10 Use the blending brush to soften these marks, working in the direction in which the hair lies. This process will give these marks a streaky appearance that helps to emphasize the illusion of hair.

11 Use the tip of a dry 1" (2.5 cm) paintbrush to pick up a little unmixed Van Dyke brown paint from the palette. Dab the brush on a cloth to remove excess paint. Holding the brush loosely in your hand, flog the paint surface with the tips of the bristles. Work across the surface in the direction of the hair. This 'flogging' process gives the surface a stippled appearance that resembles short hairs.

12 Allow the surface to dry thoroughly; this may take up to two days depending on conditions – check for dryness by touching it lightly with the tip of your finger. When completely dry, seal with a coat of polyurethane varnish.

▲ *Faux leopard skin works equally well on small objects. Here a delicate, scaled-down leopard print transforms a slim mirror frame into a gorgeous dressing table accessory.*

▶ *Go wild and use a color that is entirely 'wrong' to create fantasy leopard print. The same basic technique has been used for this romantic pink version; the glazes have been mixed from alizarin crimson and white.*

DECORATING TERRA-COTTA POTS

Add three-dimensional detailing to plain terra-cotta flowerpots with dainty motifs made from modeling clay. Use craft paints to color the motifs and to paint background details on the pot surface.

Plain, unglazed terra-cotta flowerpots, though attractive in themselves, are perfect candidates for a touch of decorative detailing. By adding small motifs made from modeling clay, in shapes such as flowers, hearts or leaves, you can enhance the decorative value of the pot while still retaining the charm of the original material.

Self-hardening modeling clay, available from art and craft stores, is an ideal material to use for the pot motifs. It looks like terra-cotta, is easy to handle and dries quickly. All you need to do is shape your motifs, paint them and glue them in place.

You can use the simple clay motifs shown on the following pages as inspiration, or create your own designs. Food cutters are useful for shaping the clay and are a good source of design ideas. The instructions show you how to decorate a pot with a simple trailing ivy motif, but the basic technique is the same for any design.

The motifs look effective on both plain terra-cotta and painted pots. It's best to seal painted pots, especially those destined for outdoor use, with a tough varnish; seal them inside and out after painting.

▼ *A set of small pots, softly colorwashed and decorated with ivy leaf motifs, make perfect containers for displaying bright and colorful spring flowers. The trailing stems are hand-painted onto the pots once the motifs are in place.*

MAKING TERRA-COTTA POT MOTIFS

YOU WILL NEED

- ➤ Unglazed terra-cotta pot
- ➤ Scrubbing brush and soft cloth
- ➤ Disposable plate or old dish
- ➤ Craft paints
- ➤ Paintbrush

- ➤ Clear acrylic sealer
- ➤ Self-hardening modeling clay, in terra-cotta color
- ➤ Spray mister (optional)
- ➤ Cardboard template or food cutters

- ➤ Small craft knife, cutting mat
- ➤ Artist's brush
- ➤ Ceramic adhesive
- ➤ Low-tack masking tape (optional)
- ➤ Varnish (optional)

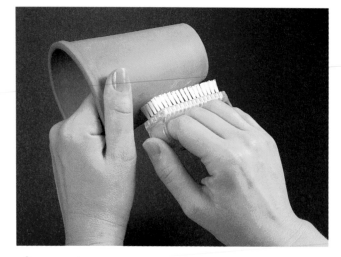

1 Scrub the terra-cotta pot with soapy water to remove any dirt; if the pot is stained, try scrubbing it with a mild bleach solution – wear gloves to protect your hands. Rinse the pot well, then allow it to dry thoroughly. Wipe it with a soft cloth to remove dust before painting.

2 Dilute the paint with equal amounts of water and brush it on the pot; colorwash the inside of the pot to below soil level. Allow the pot to dry, then apply a coat of clear acrylic sealer inside and out. Alternatively, paint the pot with undiluted paint; or leave it unpainted, and seal.

▲ *To make the carrot motifs shown here, roll the clay into a fat sausage, tapering one end into a rounded point. Make the carrot tops by cutting and rolling thinner strips of clay.*

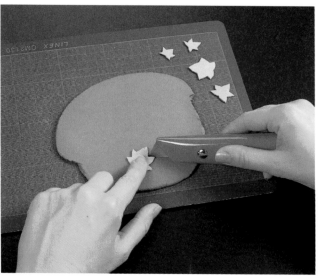

3 Knead a small amount of modeling clay until it is pliable; use a spray mister to dampen it if the clay starts to dry out. Roll out the clay to a thickness of 1/8" to 1/4" (3 to 6 mm), depending on the desired thickness of your finished motifs. Cut a template of your chosen shape(s) from card; place it on the clay and cut around it to make the desired number of motifs. Alternatively, you can use a food cutter.

Paint extra details directly on the surface of the decorated pot, if desired. Here, stems have been added to form trailing ivy: use the tip of a small artist's paintbrush to paint in small, curved lines, linking the ivy leaf motifs. Allow to dry.

4 Scratch the back of the motifs with a knife to create texture for the adhesive. Lay the first motif in position on the pot, and gently press it to fit the curve of the pot. Mark any extra pattern details, such as the veins for the leaf, then draw around the motif with a pencil to mark its position; remove the motif. Repeat the process for each motif, then allow them to dry in a warm place for 24 hours.

5 Use an artist's brush to paint the clay motifs in the desired colors. Paint in details, such as the leaf veins, once the main colors are dry. Allow the motifs to dry thoroughly.

6 Spread a little adhesive on the back of the first motif and within the pencil outline on the pot; if part of the motif is to stand above the rim, apply the adhesive to the contact area only. When the adhesive becomes tacky, secure the motif in place on the pot. Hold large or heavy motifs in place with tape, if necessary, until dry. Wipe off excess adhesive before it dries.

125

Simple motifs, such as flowers, crowns and hearts, complement the charm of the pots beautifully. Here, unpainted clay motifs have been glued to the pots, then the pots and their motifs have been colorwashed. The diluted paint sinks into the porous surface, making the motifs look like part of the original pottery.

You can create a variety of effects using a selection of food cutters. Star and heart cutters in different sizes are all you need – even the daisy motif was adapted from a star-shaped cutter, with the flower center formed from a small ball of clay.

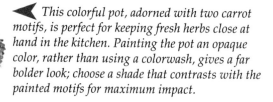

This colorful pot, adorned with two carrot motifs, is perfect for keeping fresh herbs close at hand in the kitchen. Painting the pot an opaque color, rather than using a colorwash, gives a far bolder look; choose a shade that contrasts with the painted motifs for maximum impact.

WIND CHIMES

*Make an attractive and melodic wind chime from
lengths of copper pipe, strung from glass-beaded threads
that shimmer prettily as they catch the light.*

The wind chime consists of six lengths of copper pipe, hung on beaded nylon threads from a hexagonal support. The pipes – or chimes – are cut to different lengths so they sound a range of tones. They are grouped in a circle around a central beaded thread that carries a 'flyer', a small disc that catches the breeze, and a 'striker', a wooden ball that strikes the chimes.

You can buy the copper plumbing pipe at home improvement centers and plumbing supply stores. Some retailers will cut it to length for you, or you can cut it yourself,

using a hacksaw or a pipe cutter. Medium-density fiberboard (MDF) is used for the support and flyer; it is also available at home improvement centers. For the wind chime featured here, the MDF is given an attractive verdigris finish, using green paints and copper wax, so it complements the piping.

Use nylon fishing line to support the chimes, striker and flyer; it is stronger than cotton or nylon thread, translucent, and fine enough to pass through even the tiniest beads. You can buy it at craft stores, which also offer a wide selection of beads.

▲ *Soothing to the ear
and a visual delight,
this wind chime is easy
to make from slim copper
pipe, MDF and a selection
of glass beads. Hang it in
the window where it will
catch the breeze and
sparkle in the sunlight.*

127

MAKING A COPPER PIPE WIND CHIME

YOU WILL NEED

- ➤ Copper plumbing pipe, 7/8" (2.2 cm) diameter
- ➤ Hacksaw or pipe cutter
- ➤ Tracing paper and pencil
- ➤ Medium-density fiberboard (MDF), 1/4" and 1/2" (6 mm and 1.3 cm) thick
- ➤ Hand saw
- ➤ Sandpaper, medium grade and fine grade
- ➤ Wood and metal drill bits, 3/32"
- ➤ Latex paint, in sage green
- ➤ Wood ball, 2" (5 cm) in diameter

- ➤ Paintbrush
- ➤ Copper wax
- ➤ Soft cloth
- ➤ Acrylic paint, in emerald green
- ➤ Old toothbrush
- ➤ Matte spray varnish
- ➤ Masking tape
- ➤ Hammer and nail set
- ➤ Wood block, small wood slats and nails
- ➤ Steel wool, fine grade
- ➤ Nylon fishing line
- ➤ Assorted beads
- ➤ Copper ring

Cutting out

From copper plumbing pipe Cut 6 lengths of copper pipe to the following measurements: 20" (51 cm), 18" (46 cm), 16" (40.5 cm), 14" (35.5 cm), 12" (30.5 cm) and 10" (25.5 cm).

Using a pipe cutter

Hold the pipe cutter firmly in your hand, and adjust the grip to fit the copper pipe. Turn the pipe toward you, inside the cutter, and continue to turn until it cuts through the pipe.

1 Trace the template on page 130 and cut it out. Lay it on the 1/4" (6 mm) thick MDF, and draw around it with a pencil; this will be the flyer. Enlarge the template to twice its size, using a grid or a photocopier; cut it out and lay it on the 1/2" (1.3 cm) MDF. Draw around the enlarged template and transfer the position of the holes; this will be the support.

2 Cut out both MDF shapes along the marked outlines, using a hand saw. Smooth all the cut edges of each shape, using sandpaper.

3 Drill one hole at each pencil mark on the MDF support, using a 3/32" wood drill bit. Drill a single hole in the flyer, close to one corner point. Sand the surfaces to remove any splinters near the drilled holes, and to prepare the surface for painting.

4 Paint the support, the flyer and the wood ball striker with sage green paint, and allow to dry. Use your fingertips to rub copper wax lightly over the painted shapes, allowing the green to still show through. Remove any excess wax with a clean, soft cloth; buff the surface to a sheen.

5 Dilute some emerald green acrylic paint with water. Spatter the paint across the surface of the three painted shapes by running your thumb or small dowel across the bristle of an old toothbrush. Allow to dry, then seal all surfaces with a coat of spray varnish.

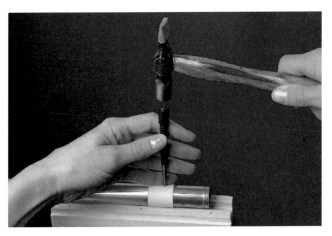

6 Wrap each length of pipe with 4 layers of masking tape, about 2" (5 cm) from one end. Mark tape 2" (5 cm) from end of each pipe; punch an indentation at the mark with a hammer and nail set or nail. Nail two small wood slats to a wooden block and sit the pipe between them. Place the metal drill bit on the dent in the pipe, and drill through and out of the other side. Drill all six pipes.

7 Remove the masking tape from each length of pipe. Smooth down any sharp edges, using fine-grade sandpaper. Polish the pipes to a soft sheen, using fine-grade steel wool.

8 Cut six lengths of nylon fishing line, approximately 24" (61 cm) long. Thread the lengths of nylon through the holes in the pipes. Thread assorted beads onto each end of the nylon strands – to a length of 2" to 3" (5 to 7.5 cm) – so that the beads sit equally on each side of the drilled holes.

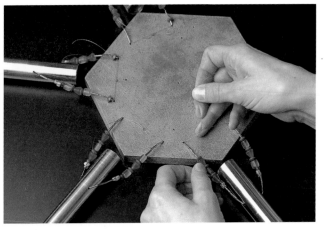

9 Push the nylon thread ends up through the holes marked in red on the enlarged template, so that one pipe lies at each corner point. Cross the thread ends on the top side of the support, then thread them back down through the holes and secure the ends on the underside with a knot. Trim off the thread ends. Hang pipes in sequence, according to length.

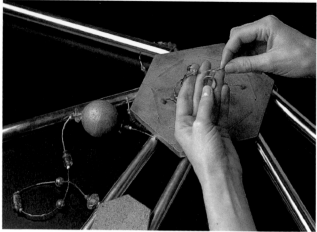

10 Cut a 40" (102 cm) length of nylon fishing line, and thread one end through the hole in the flyer; secure with a knot. Thread beads onto the nylon line in the desired arrangement, until you have covered about 16" (40.5 cm) of it. Thread the striker, then continue threading beads for a further 8" (20.5 cm) or so. Take the thread up through the central hole in the support. Hold up the wind chime and check the position of the striker; adjust by adding or removing beads.

11 Thread a length of nylon, approximately 24" (61 cm) long, down through one of the four remaining holes and up through an adjacent hole, so both ends lie on the top side of the support. Repeat to thread the remaining two holes with a second length of nylon. Thread an equal number of beads, in the desired arrangement, onto the four nylon strands, plus the center strand. Gather all the strands together and tie a double knot. Loop the threads above the knot, and tie on a copper ring for hanging the wind chime. Trim off the excess nylon line.

◀ *Try designing your own unique wind chimes, using materials of your choice. Here, shells and smooth colored glass, collected from a walk on the beach, make a delightful wind chime that catches the light. The chimes are strung using loops of thin copper wire, passed through holes drilled in the shells, and wrapped around the glass pieces. They are hung from a circle of twisted bonsai wire. Strengthen the circle by twisting the bonsai wire over itself, and support it with four arms of wire, gathered at the top and coiled to create a hook.*

TEMPLATE FOR WIND CHIME SUPPORT AND FLYER

CUTWORK PAPER LAMPSHADES

Light up a corner of your room with a pretty lampshade that diffuses the light through dainty cutout shapes. These innovative shades are surprisingly easy to make.

A cutwork paper lampshade is the perfect choice when you want subtle, indirect lighting with patches of brighter light twinkling through. The effect is achieved by cutting along design lines drawn on paper, then pushing these parts in or out slightly so that the light can shine through. You can add extra detail by using a thick needle or other pointed object to remove areas of the pattern.

A cutout lampshade is made from thick paper, which is glued onto a lightbulb ring frame. It's important to use thick paper as it holds its shape – a good weight is 10½ oz (315 g). Suitable paper is available from stationery and art supply stores; the lightbulb rings from craft stores or by mail order.

The pattern on page 133 is for a shade measuring approximately 9" (23 cm) across the base. Although paper shades are stronger than they might appear, do not use any bulb stronger than 60 watts and allow good ventilation around the shade.

▲ *The play of light enhances the dainty heart, tulip and leaf design on this cream paper cutwork lampshade. Not too intricate, but extremely effective, the design is a perfect choice for a country-style lampshade.*

MAKING A CUTWORK LAMPSHADE

1 Trace or photocopy the lampshade pattern on page ➤ 133, three times, then cut it out. Overlap and tape the sections together along the straight edges, to make the complete pattern.

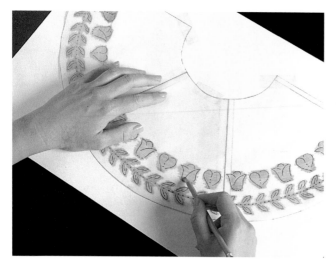

2 Rub over the design areas, using a soft pencil on the back of the pattern. Lay the pattern, right side up, on the sheet of paper and tape it in place. Lightly trace around the lampshade pattern outline and along the design lines, using a pencil.

3 Lay the paper with its traced design on a cutting mat or sheet of thick card. Cut around the marked lines of the design, using a craft knife.

4 Stab through the dots, using a thick needle or metal skewer (as shown), to form the stem for the leaves and the details on the hearts and flowers.

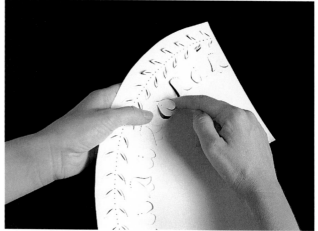

5 Gently erase the pencil lines, taking care when rubbing over the cut points. Cut out the shade. Working from the wrong side, gently push the cut shapes outward.

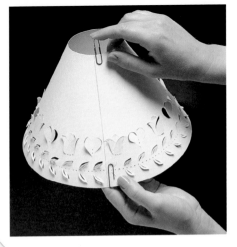

6 Cut a ⅝" (1.5 cm) wide strip from the end of the crêpe paper roll. Wrap the strip around the outer ring of the bulb frame, securing the ends with a dab of adhesive.

7 Roll the shade to form a cone shape and hold the overlap in place with paper clips at the top and bottom edges. Check the fit of the bulb frame and adjust the overlap as necessary. Apply a thin line of adhesive down one straight edge and glue the shade together, securing the edges with paper clips while the adhesive dries.

Black lines show cut lines. Dotted lines show pierced sections

8 Spread a little adhesive around the outer ring of the bulb frame. Turn the shade upside down and wedge the ring down to rest just inside the narrow end of the shade. Allow to dry.

LAMPSHADE PATTERN

Leaf Motif Design

Cascading leaves cut on pale green paper create a stylish finish. Use the leaf motif below to create the look. The bold lines indicate the cutting lines. Enlarge or reduce the shape, as you wish, to vary the effect.

LEAF PATTERN

Black lines show cut lines

Scalloped edges

To add a scalloped edge to your lampshade, extend the two straight sides of the pattern by ¾" (2 cm). Lightly draw lines parallel to the top and bottom curves. Draw even scallops along both edges. Cut around the shapes, using a craft knife.

If you don't feel confident about cutting intricate designs, try simple shapes such as these geometric ones, to liven up a plain shade almost instantly.

This delicate cutwork lampshade with its pretty scalloped edges casts a subtle pattern around a room.

KITCHEN CHALKBOARD

This handy chalkboard is a decorative and practical accessory for your home. Simple to make from MDF, you can use it to jot down reminders for yourself or messages to your friends and family.

Chalkboards have progressed from the schoolroom to find a new lease on life in the modern home. Practical, simple to make and easy to use, they are a boon in the busy kitchen or home office. A wall-mounted chalkboard can be used to list 'out of stock' groceries, to leave messages and to flag important dates. A large board will provide a useful drawing surface in a child's room, and small children can practice their writing skills.

The board is made of medium-density fiberboard (MDF), cut into shape using a jigsaw. Our chalkboard measures just 19¾" x 15¾" (50 x 40 cm), but you can make it any size and adapt the dimensions to fit your wall space. The writing area is created using special blackboard paint, which is available at home improvement centers. The finished board has an optional shelf for holding chalks.

The board can be painted in a single color, shades of the same color or clever contrasts. Customize your board with drilled holes, applied motifs or decoupage. Decorated chalkboards make ideal gifts.

▲ *This simple chalkboard is the perfect accessory for a kitchen or hallway. Use it to make notes or quick lists, or hang it beside the telephone to jot down numbers or messages.*

135

MAKING THE CHALKBOARD

Measuring and cutting out

For the backboard Cut a square from 5/8" (1.5 cm) MDF 4" (10 cm) bigger than the desired finished size to accommodate the curve at the top.

For the shelf Cut a rectangle from the 3/8" (1 cm) MDF half the size of the backboard.

1 For the backboard, draw a 15¾" (40 cm) wide 20" (51 cm) high rectangle on the 5/8" (15 cm) thick MDF. Mark the curve at the top using a saucer as a template; center the saucer along the marked top edge of the board, as shown, and draw around the upper half of the saucer to form a semicircle. Cut out the backboard along the marked lines using the jigsaw; sand the cut edges.

2 For the shelf, draw a 15¾" x 2¼" (40 x 6 cm) rectangle on the 3/8" (10 cm) thick MDF. Round the front corners of the shelf using a small jar as a template; place it in each corner and draw around the edge. Cut out the shelf with the jigsaw, following the marked lines. Sand the cut edges.

3 Mark a line 2" (5 cm) from the bottom of the backboard. Spread wood glue along the back of the shelf and press it firmly onto the board, just above the marked pencil line. Larger boards may require nails in addition to the glue to hold the shelf in place; hammer in a row from the back of the board and countersink them with the nail set.

4 Center a small drinking glass on the front of the backboard, just beneath the curved area at the top edge; draw around the glass, using a pencil. Mark the center of the circle with a pencil, then use a metal ruler to measure and mark a point every 3/8" (1 cm) around the edge.

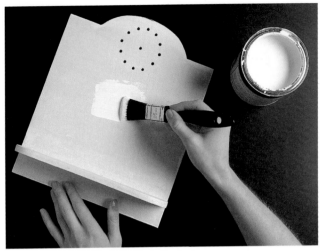

5 Drill a hole at the marked centerpoint of the circle; drill holes at the marked points around the edge of the circle. Sand away any rough edges.

6 Apply two coats of water-based wood primer to the front and back; allow the first coat to dry thoroughly before you apply the second coat. Sand the surface smooth between coats, if necessary. Allow to dry.

7 Apply two coats of latex paint to the front and back, allowing the first coat to dry before applying the second; avoid filling the drilled holes with paint. Allow to dry overnight.

8 Mark the blackboard area in the center with strips of painter's tape. Press down the edges of the tape firmly with a fingernail.

9 Apply two or three coats of the blackboard paint to the masked-off area. When the paint is thoroughly dry, peel away the masking tape to leave a crisply edged black rectangle.

▶ *You can make a fun blackboard for a small child. Adapt the size as desired and then cut out and paint the board without attaching the shelf. Decorate the border around the blackboard or let your child have a go!*

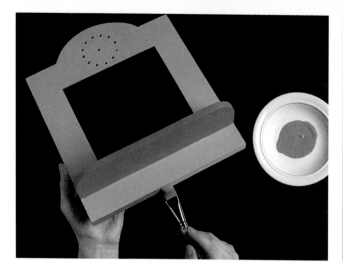

10 Add a slightly shaded effect to the blackboard by applying two coats of a darker shade of paint to the edges of the backboard and the shelf, allowing the paint to dry thoroughly between each coat.

11 On the back of the blackboard, mark a point approximately ¾" (2 cm) down from the center of the top curved edge. Attach a small picture hanger at this point to hang the blackboard on the wall.

◄ *Create a strong Southwest-style design by cutting motifs from metal sheet or foil using pinking shears. Use a coin or small jar as a template for the circles, and simply cut strips to go around the blackboard area. Secure the motifs to the frame using tacks or brads.*

DECORATIVE DOOR KNOBS

Liven up a plain cupboard or chest of drawers by creating your own enchanting door knobs using copper wire, colored beads and clear polyester resin.

If you can't find the right door knobs to finish off a room, or you are looking for something out of the ordinary to add interest to a plain cupboard or chest of drawers, you can use the following technique to make original resin door knobs in an array of exciting designs.

The molds that form the shape of the knobs are small and inexpensive aluminum cookie molds, which can be found in a variety of shapes. You simply fill the mold with copper wire spirals and beads, set in a long-shanked bolt, pour in polyester resin mixed with hardener and allow to set. The shapes can then be removed and the mold used again for another design.

The possibilities for decorating the door knobs are endless. All kinds of small, decorative items work effectively. Small seashells set into the resin would be perfect for a bathroom cupboard, and small plastic soldiers, cars or bright plastic flowers for a child's room.

When pouring the resin into the cookie mold, take care to completely cover any ends of wire or metal with the resin, as these could be sharp if left sticking out the back of the knob. If this is unavoidable, be sure to trim off any wire ends with wire cutters, and sand down the remaining stump for safety.

Small aluminum cookie molds can be obtained in a variety of shapes and sizes in the housewares department or at specialty baking stores. Copper wire and polyester resin are both available at craft stores, and long-shanked bolts from hardware and home improvement centers.

▶ *A glittering crystal door knob, made from beads, wire and resin, adds a modern twist to this pretty pine cupboard.*

MAKING A STARBURST DOOR KNOB

YOU WILL NEED

- ➤ 20 to 24-gauge copper wire
- ➤ Wire cutters
- ➤ Needlenose pliers
- ➤ Glass or ceramic beads in assorted colors and sizes
- ➤ Aluminum cookie mold

- ➤ Long-shanked bolt with nut
- ➤ Polyester resin and hardener
- ➤ Freezer paper
- ➤ Sandpaper, fine grade

1 Cut a length of 1/16" (1.5 mm) copper wire approximately 24" (61 cm) long. Use a pair of needlenose pliers to hold one end tight and bend the wire around the nose to form a tight coil.

2 Hold the opposite sides of the coil between thumb and forefinger and gently push the center of the coil toward you to form a spiral or spring. Leave the center of the coil flat so the spiral will balance on a flat surface.

➤ *Experiment with bead colors and wire shapes to create your own individual door knob designs. Different style inlays will suit different locations in your home.*

3 Thread the amber-colored beads along the spiral, easing them toward its center.

4 Introduce a second color to the spiral with more beads, once again easing them toward its center. When the spiral is almost covered, check it against the depth of your mold and space the beads accordingly.

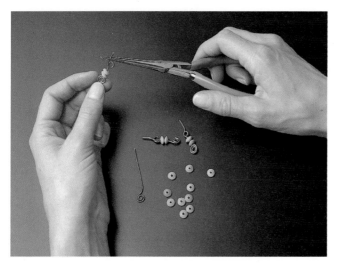

5 Cut four lengths of wire to about 2" (5 cm) long and use the pliers to make a small coil at one end of each length. Thread two or three beads (according to mold depth and bead size) along each wire and form a small loop at each end.

6 Arrange the wires evenly around the edge of the mold, and set the beaded spiral in the center. Make sure that the wires are at least 3/16" (4.5 mm) below the top of the mold so the ends will be covered with resin.

7 Remove the nut from the long-shanked bolt and position the bolt in the center of the spiral.

8 Mix the polyester resin and hardener, following manufacturer's directions. The amount required will depend on your mold and bead size, so start by mixing 1/2 cup (125 mL) of resin with hardener, and mix more if necessary.

➤ *Let your imagination run wild with different beads and other accessories for your door knobs. As long as the items are small enough to be covered with the resin, anything goes.*

9 Place the mold on a piece of freezer paper, check the bead and wire arrangement, and pour the mixture slowly into the mold; avoid disturbing the arrangement or spilling any resin on the bolt stem. Allow the resin to cure for approximately 2 1/2 hours.

10 Ease the shape out of the mold when dry; the resin should not be sticky to the touch. You may need to pour boiling water over the back of the mold to help ease it out. Smooth any sharp edges, using fine sandpaper.

11 Snip off any protruding wire ends as close to the surface as you can, using wire cutters, and sand the sharp stumps with fine sandpaper.

▲ *Try using coins in the base of the mold; attractive foreign coins add an intriguing touch. Consider cutting the shank off the back of decorative buttons. Use your own imagination for unlimited fun.*

◀ *Use an assortment of knobs on a small storage chest for an eye-catching effect. The beads and wire spirals gleam like jewels when light catches the crystal resin.*

INDEX

Photograph Acknowledgments: Front cover (main) Creative Publishing international, (cl) Eaglemoss/Steven Pam, (bl) Eaglemoss/Gareth Sambridge, 5-6 Robert Harding Syndication/Homes & Ideas/Dominic Blackmore, 7-12 Creative Publishing international, 13 Robert Harding Syndication/Homes & Ideas/Dominic Blackmore, 14 Eaglemoss/Lizzie Orme, 15 Creative Publishing International, 16(tl) Eaglemoss/Steve Tanner, (tr) Robert Harding Syndication/Homes & Gardens/Gavin Kingcome, (bl) Robert Harding Syndication/Ideal Home/Lucinda Symons, 17-23 Eaglemoss/Lizzie Orme, 24(cl) Elizabeth Whiting & Associates/Andreas von Einsiedel, (br) Elizabeth Whiting & Associates/Michael Dunne, 25-27 Creative Publishing international, 28(tl) Creative Publishing international, (tr,b) Eaglemoss/Lizzie Orme, 29 Eaglemoss/Lizzie Orme, 30-31 Eaglemoss/Graham Rae, 32 Eaglemoss/Lizzie Orme, 33-45 Eaglemoss/Ian Howes, 47-48 Eaglemoss/Lizzie Orme, 49 Marie Claire Idées/Becquet/Lancrenon, 50-52 Eaglemoss/Steven Pam, 53-55 Eaglemoss/Julian Busselle, 56(cr) Textra, (bl) Osborne and Little, 57-60 Eaglemoss/Lizzie Orme, 61-64 Eaglemoss/Steven Pam, 65 Ariadne Holland, 66-67 Eaglemoss/Simon Page-Richie, 68(tl) Elizabeth Whiting & Associates/Brian Harrison, (tr) Robert Harding Syndication/Country Homes & Interiors/Bill Batten, (b) Eaglemoss/Simon Page-Ritchie, 69-74 Eaglemoss/Jon Bouchier, 75-77 Eaglemoss/Paul Bricknell, 78(tl) Elizabeth Whiting & Associates/Jean-Paul Bonhommet, (bl) Eaglemoss/Adrian Taylor, (br) Robert Harding Syndication/IPC/Ideal Home, 79-80 Eaglemoss/Graham Rae, 81 Eaglemoss/Gareth Sambidge, 82-83 Eaglemoss/Graham Rae, 84(bl) Eaglemoss/Paul Bricknell, 85 Robert Harding Syndication/IPC/Woman & Home, 86-87 Creative Publishing international, 88(tr) Robert Harding Syndication/IPC/Homes & Ideas, (bl) Eaglemoss/Lizzie Orme, (br) Robert Harding Syndication/IPC/Homes & Ideas, 89 Jane Churchill, 90-92 Eaglemoss/Jon Bouchier, 92(bl) Robert Harding Syndication/Homes & Gardens/Jan Baldwin, 93-96 Eaglemoss/Paul Bricknell, 96(b) Eaglemoss/Gareth Sambidge, 97-99 Eaglemoss/Graham Rae, 100 Eaglemoss/Gareth Sambidge, 101-102 Creative Publishing international, 103 Robert Harding Syndication/Country Homes & Interiors/Andreas von Einsiedel, 104-105 Eaglemoss/Lizzie Orme, 106(t,cl,br) Artex, Blue Hawk, (cr) Copley Décor, 107-109 Eaglemoss/Graham Rae, 110(t) Marie Claire Idées/Chabaneix/Richard, (bl) Robert Harding Syndication/IPC/Ideal Home, (br) Eaglemoss/Graham Rae, 111 Creative Publishing international, 112-113 Eaglemoss/Lizzie Orme, 114(tl) Robert Harding Syndication/IPC/Ideal Home, (tr) Marie Claire Idées/Hussenot/Lancrenon/Chastres, (bl) Elizabeth Whiting & Associates/Di Lewis, (br) Marie Claire Idées/Giaume/de Lamotte, 115 Eaglemoss/Graham Rae, 116-118 Eaglemoss/Paul Bricknell, 119-122 Eaglemoss/Graham Rae, 123-126 Eaglemoss/Steven Pam, 126(tl) Eaglemoss/Steve Tanner, (cr) Eaglemoss/Graham Rae, 127-130 Eaglemoss/Ian Howes, 131-133 Eaglemoss/Graham Rae, 134(t) Eaglemoss/Graham Rae, (bl) Marie Claire Maison/Verger/Jacqueline, (br) Robert Harding Syndication/Country Homes & Interiors/Tim Imrie, 135-138 Eaglemoss/Graham Rae, 139-142 Eaglemoss/Ian Howes, 140(bl) Eaglemoss/Graham Rae, 142(cr) Eaglemoss/Graham Rae, (bl) Eaglemoss/Jo Bourne, Back cover (tl) Marie Claire Idées/Chabaneix/Richard, (c) Robert Harding Syndication/Homes & Ideas/Dominic Blackmore, (br) Eaglemoss/Gareth Sambridge.

Illustrations: John Hutchinson

Creative Publishing international offers a variety of how-to books. For information write:
Creative Publishing international
Subscriber Books
5900 Green Oak Drive
Minnetonka, MN 55343
1-800-328-3895

Library of Congress Cataloging-in-Publication Data
Decorative touches : 35 step-by-step projects.
    p. cm.
    Includes index.
    ISBN 0-86573-334-1 (sc)
    1. Handicraft. 2. House furnishings. 3. Interior decoration.
I. Creative Publishing International.
TT157.D388 1999
645--DC21   98-44470